# CLASSIC MAYA PLACE NAMES

DAVID STUART and STEPHEN HOUSTON

Dumbarton Oaks Research Library and Collection       Washington, D.C. 1994

# Note

In this monograph we employ glyphic conventions devised by George Stuart
for his *Research Reports on Ancient Maya Writing,* published by the Center for
Maya Research. Close transcriptions of Maya glyphs appear in boldface type:
logographs in uppercase, phonetic syllables in lowercase. Transliterations,
which correspond to Mayan words and not to their glyphic referents, occur
in italics.

Library of Congress Cataloging-in-Publication Data

Stuart, David, 1965–
    Classic Maya place names / David Stuart and Stephen Houston.
      p.   cm.—(Studies in pre-Columbian art & archaeology ; no.
33)
    Includes bibliographical references.
    ISBN 0-88402-209-9
    1. Mayas—Writing.  2. Mayas—Names.  3. Names, Geographical—
Central America.  4. Names, Geographical—Mexico.  I. Houston,
Stephen D.  II. Title.  III. Series.
F1435.3.W75S78   1993
917.2′0014—dc20                     92-30114
                                          CIP

# Contents

# List of Figures

# Preface

The first draft of this study, outlining the identifications of place glyphs for various sites, was written and circulated among several of our colleagues in 1986. An oral version was also presented at the November 1989 meetings of the American Society for Ethnohistory. The scope of the present work is larger than these earlier versions, however, including many more examples of place glyphs and drawing on more diverse sets of evidence. The evolution of this work was constantly fueled by rapid developments in Maya epigraphy, for as each draft neared completion, new findings compelled further revision.

We are greatly indebted to the many friends and colleagues who contributed their time and encouragement during the gestation of this work. Ian Graham showed his customary generosity with his fine drawings produced under the auspices of the Corpus of Maya Hieroglyphic Inscriptions at the Peabody Museum of Harvard University. Victoria Bricker, Michael Coe, Nikolai Grube, Linda Schele, Karl Taube, Elizabeth Boone, and an anonymous reviewer provided several suggestions that were both helpful and greatly appreciated; they strongly urged us to publish our results as quickly as possible. Although unavoidable delays occurred, we have attempted to follow their advice. However, as our findings have already filtered into the epigraphic community and even further afield without a corresponding publication, some confusion regarding proper citation has resulted (e.g., Marhenke 1989: 59). We apologize for misunderstandings that were due to the publishing delay. Here we finally offer the place name evidence in a readily accessible, complete form, which we hope will provide a good resource for future study and debate in the field.

# Introduction

Despite the progress of the past twenty years in bringing to light the historical contents of Maya inscriptions, much remains to be done. Among many other little-known subjects, that of Maya geography is only vaguely understood, notwithstanding Heinrich Berlin's (1958) identification of "Emblem Glyphs" for sites. Since Berlin's work, scholars have used Emblem Glyphs specifically to address questions of Maya political geography. Joyce Marcus' (1976) Dumbarton Oaks volume *Emblem and State in the Classic Maya Lowlands* broke new ground in this area, and the recent publication of the School of American Research Seminar on Classic political history (Culbert 1991) demonstrates a continuing interest in ancient Maya geopolitics. The limitation such scholars faced, however, was one of inadequate data. Unable to go beyond the study of Emblem Glyphs, now recognized as general references to political units (Mathews 1991), these studies could not discuss the actual features of the ancient Maya landscape. Therefore, although most efforts in Maya decipherment have focused on the "when" and "who" of historical and ritual events, we hope in this monograph to shed light on the previously murky question of "where."

We suggest that specific place names do exist in Maya inscriptions and that by identifying them we may shed considerable light on both old and new questions about the Maya. Precise place names bring the study of the ancient landscape into a much sharper focus. No longer must broad political divisions (Mathews 1985) substitute for actual geographic locations and features in our study of the ancient Maya. By studying place names, several important issues can be addressed by future research. For example, the potential exists to document the shifting borders of Maya polities, as named sites are absorbed into, or released from, the dominions of larger centers. The terminology used for the ancient place names we identify—often centered on such terms as *wits*, "hill," or *ha'*, "water"—may reveal certain aspects of how the Maya viewed the natural landscape and their relationship to it. Similar issues have arisen in the study of place names in other areas of Mesoamerica (Pohl and Byland 1990). Even so, many of the place names we identify in the inscriptions cannot be linked precisely to known sites; hopefully, further fieldwork will someday remedy this problem.

Beyond the important questions of political interaction, hierarchy, and so on, place glyphs can also be identified in numerous ritual contexts. Hieroglyphic names of parts of sites or even of individual structures reveal the locations of rituals, and these can sometimes be integrated with physical remains in the archaeological record. Even more interesting, perhaps, are the place names we associate with Maya supernaturals. This mythical landscape, attested in inscriptions and painted ceramics, appears to be as complex and varied as the places associated with historical people and events.

In this initial stage of research, however, we concentrate our discussion on how place names are identified and what glyphs can be associated with specific locales. In proposing a new category of glyphs, we necessarily delve into detailed discussion of particular hieroglyphs and the evidences for their various readings. Nonetheless, we trust that because of the broader implications involved, our audience will not be limited to specialists in Maya decipherment.

# CHAPTER 1

# Identifying Place Names in Maya Inscriptions

Our study is not the first to address the nature of locational references in Maya hieroglyphic writing. Since the last century, for instance, pages 65b–69b of the Dresden Codex (Fig. 1a–e) have been recognized as discussing thirteen places associated with the Maya rain god, Chaak (Thomas 1888; Barthel 1953; Mathews and Justeson 1984). Here and in other isolated passages of the Dresden Codex, Chaak sits on a hieroglyph or iconographic symbol referring to a specific place or environment. In the captions above these small scenes, the second glyph consistently corresponds to these locations and takes a locative preposition prefix (for *ti* or *ta,* "in, at, on"). For example, on page 65b (Fig. 1d) one frame shows Chaak seated on a sky band, while another pictures the deity atop the head of an old man (Fig. 1e). The captions above read, respectively, "Chaak (is) in the sky" and "Chaak (is) on the hill," with additional glyphs probably specifying offerings for these occasions (Kelley 1976: 109). These passages in the Dresden Codex illustrate a merging of text and image that is extremely common in Maya references to place; as we shall show later, this pattern has clear antecedents in the monuments of the Classic period.

However, the study of place references in Classic inscriptions has until now been limited to the analysis of "Emblem Glyphs" (Fig. 2), first identified by Heinrich Berlin (1958: 111) as glyphs referring in some unknown manner to specific dynasties, tutelary deities, or names of specific sites. Opting for the last of these interpretations, David Kelley (1976: 215) stated that, "On a priori grounds, there ought to be place names in the inscriptions, the Emblem Glyphs function as if they were place names, and there is no other known body of glyphs which could furnish place names; hence I regard the Emblem Glyphs as place names." Yet Kelley is only partly correct. We believe that Emblem Glyphs refer to political units that could incorporate several named sites. In this chapter, we will discuss the existence of a largely separate category of glyphs that refers more specifically to the names of sites, much in the same manner as the toponymic glyphs long known from Central Mexico and Oaxaca (Peñafiel 1885; Caso 1949).

## New Understandings of Emblem Glyphs

The study of locational references in Maya historical texts has continued apace in the years since Berlin's important recognition of Emblem Glyphs (or Emblems, as we shall occasionally call them). Although Berlin avoided assigning a precise function to Emblems, assuming that they might in some way refer to ruling dynasties, tutelary deities, or actual site names, other scholars have offered more specific interpretations. Joyce Marcus (1976: 11) stressed one part of Berlin's interpretation, arguing that Emblem Glyphs served principally as geographic references, or place names. Peter Mathews and John Justeson (1984) later clarified the meaning and composition of Emblem Glyphs, showing that they functioned primarily as *titles of rulers* having some geographic association (see also Mathews 1991).

Emblems usually comprise three elements, including a variable "main sign" that Berlin recog-

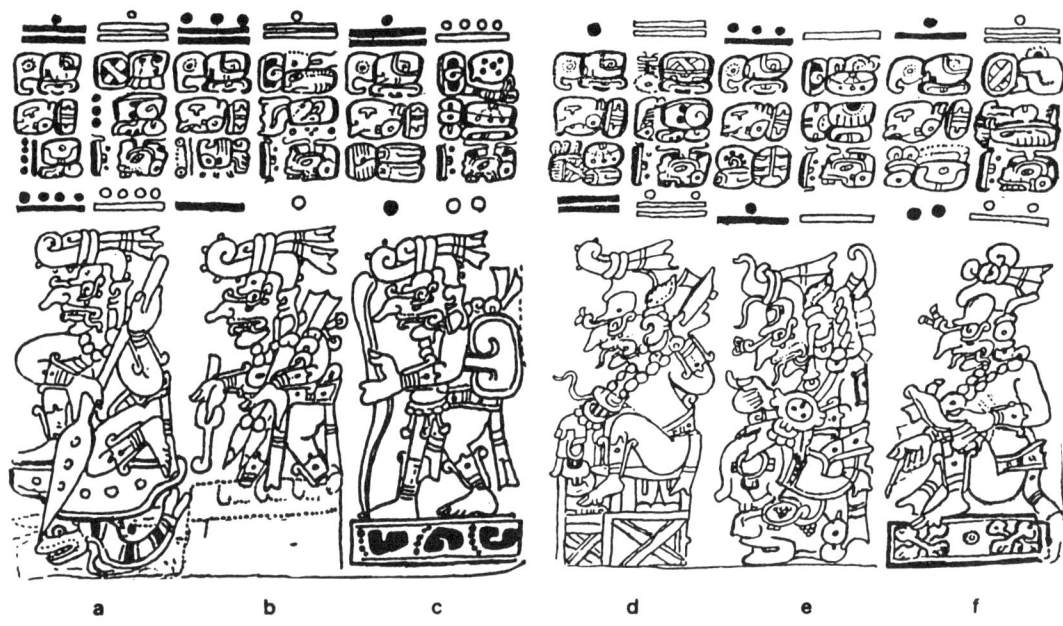

a       b       c       d       e       f

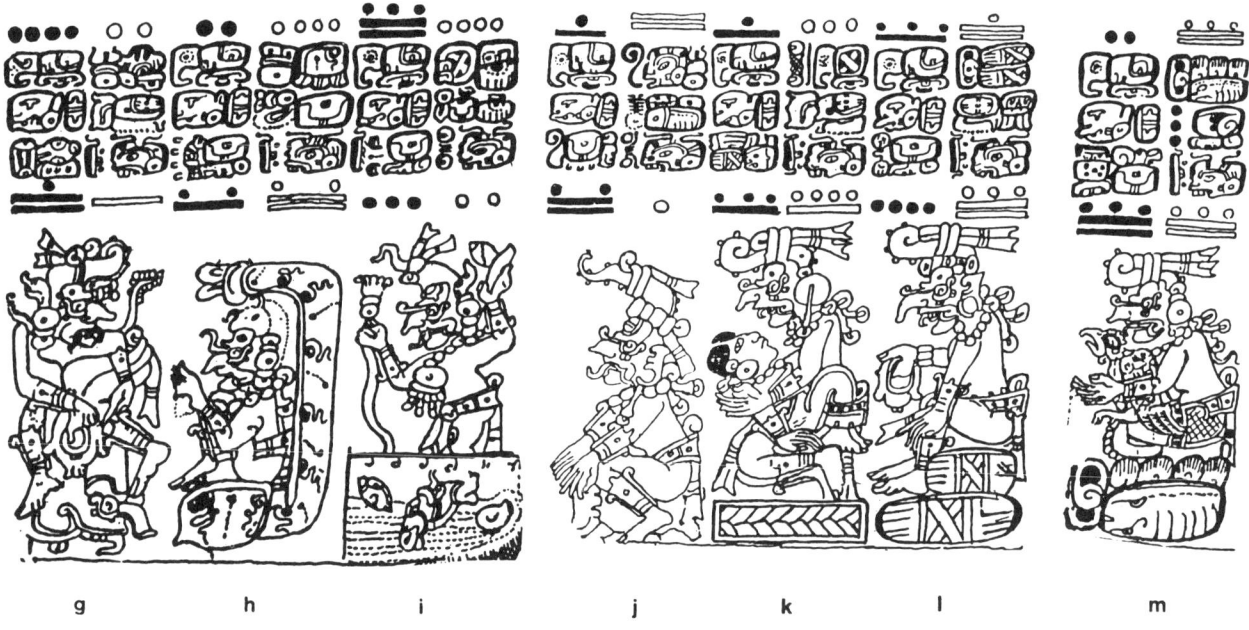

g       h       i       j       k       l       m

Fig. 1 Pages 65b to 69b of the Dresden Codex (after Villacorta and Villacorta 1930: 140, 142, 144, 146, 148).

4

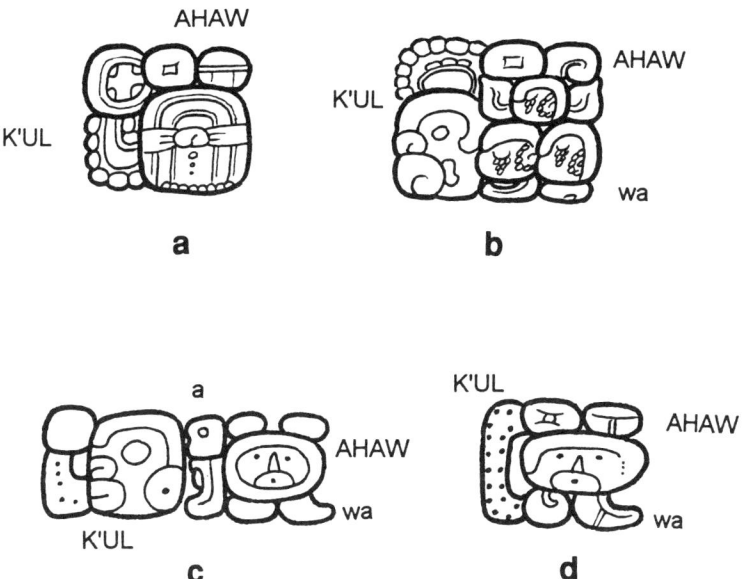

Fig. 2 Emblem Glyphs

(a) Tikal Emblem Glyph, Tikal Stela 22: A8 (after Jones and Satterthwaite 1982: fig. 33)

(b) Seibal Emblem Glyph, Seibal Hieroglyphic Stairway 1: 6 (after unpublished drawing by Ian Graham)

(c) *ch'ul ahaw* from Chichen Itza, Temple of the Initial Series: H2–I2 (after Krochok 1989: fig. 1)

(d) Chichen Itza, Temple of the One Lintel: E1 (after Krochok 1989: fig. 2).

nized as specific to certain sites. In addition to this variable element, which Mathews and Justeson (1984: 216) interpret as signifying "the political unit over which one site held dominion," a basic component of Emblem Glyphs is the honorific title *ahaw*, "lord," renderable in several ways and always read after the variable main sign. The so-called water group sign comes first (actually representing sacrificial blood), although it can be absent, particularly in inscriptions of the Early Classic period. Mathews (1991) notes that the presence or absence of this prefix does not appear to alter radically the meaning of Emblems, but we caution that the question of meaning must be based upon a precise phonetic reading for the sign, which Mathews does not discuss. The prefix seems to read **K'U,** "god," or **K'UL,** "divine, holy" (or the Cholan cognates **CH'U** or **CH'UL;** Barthel 1968; Ringle 1988). At Chichen Itza and Uxmal, "Emblem Glyphs" (Kelley 1976: fig. 72; Kowalski

1986) are in fact composed of only these two elements, *k'ul ahaw*, without the variable main sign (Fig. 2c; see Fig. 3 for the location of sites mentioned in text). We believe that this is simply a title for principal lords, and one that exists today among the Tzotzil Maya, *ch'ul 'ojow*, "holy lord" (Guiteras-Holmes 1961: 262; orthography in the original).

The understanding of Emblem Glyphs has been refined by one of the authors (D. Stuart 1985b), who has shown that the variable element of the Emblem from Yaxha (Figs. 4a–b), first identified by Justeson (1975), is read **YAX-a,** or *Yaxha'*, a term that today refers to the large lake near the archaeological site of the same name. This single example reveals that the variable main signs of Emblem Glyphs can indeed refer to places rather than to ruling families or tutelary deities. Accordingly, in its most common form the Yaxha Emblem is very likely to be read *Yaxha' Ahaw*,

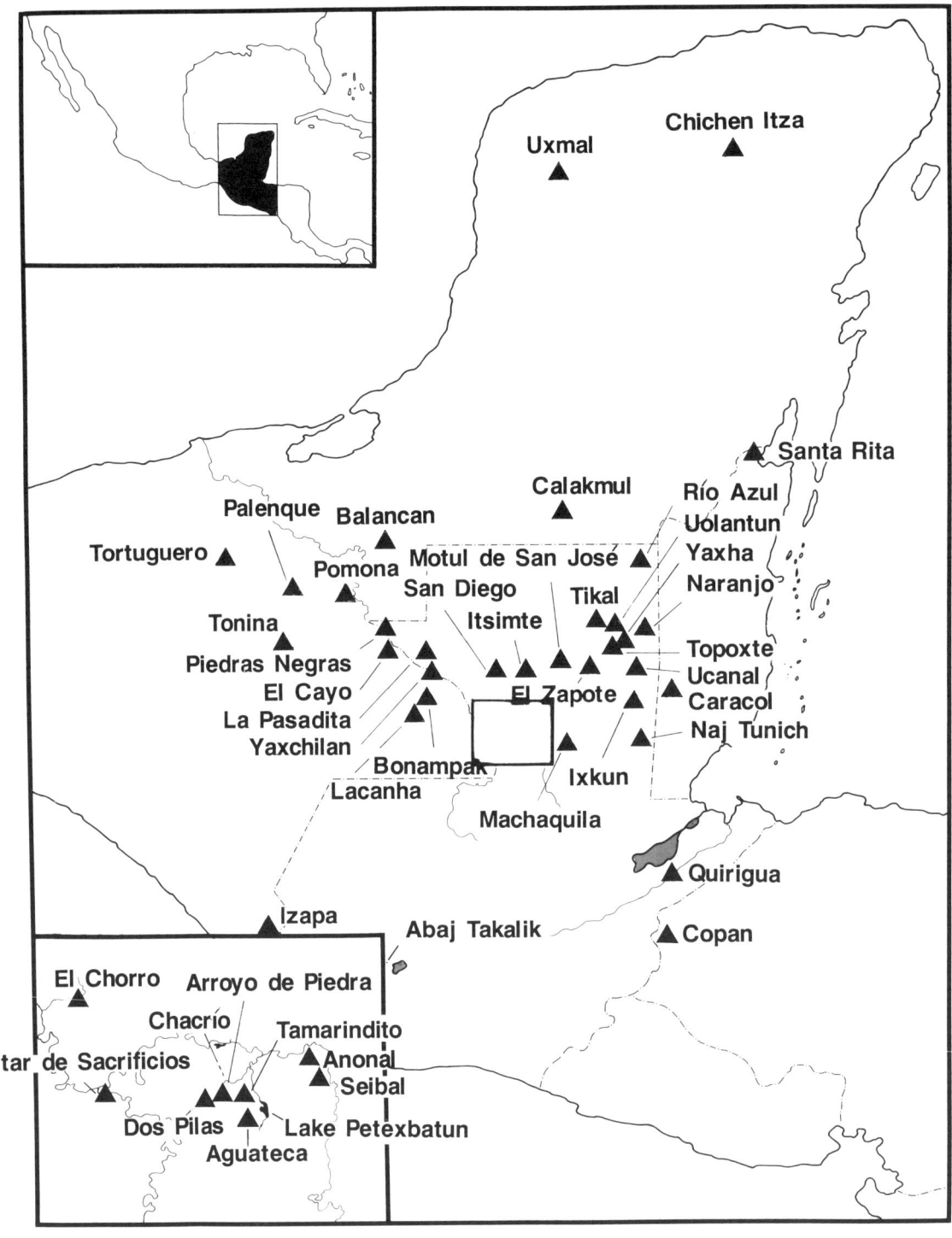

Fig. 3 Map showing sites mentioned in the text.

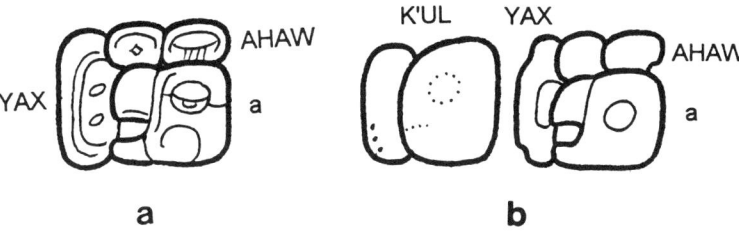

Fig. 4 Yaxha Emblem glyph

(a) *Yaxha' ahaw,* on Naranjo Stela 23: F20 (after *CMHI* 2: 60)

(b) *K'ul Yaxha' Ahaw,* from Yaxha Stela 6 (after Maler 1908a: pl. 17).

"Yaxha lord" (Fig. 4a). When the "water group" prefix is present, the full reading becomes *K'ul Yaxha' Ahaw,* "divine Yaxha lord," most probably the exclusive title of the ruler (Fig. 4b).

Despite this new phonetic reading of Emblem Glyphs, many questions remain unanswered. Why, for example, is one Emblem shared by Tikal and Dos Pilas, sites far distant from each other? And why do rulers of Yaxchilan and Palenque often use two distinct Emblem Glyphs with their names? It would seem that some Emblem Glyph main signs, although geographically variable, do not refer to specific sites—this pattern was, after all, one impetus for Mathews' and Justeson's proposal that Emblem Glyphs might allude to larger territories. In our opinion, the ambiguity is the result of insufficient decipherment, inasmuch as we have yet to understand the precise function of all Emblem Glyph main signs. Even the *Yaxha'* decipherment of the Yaxha Emblem Glyph still fails to elucidate the geographical scope of its reference. The name Yaxha might specify the lake area, as it does today, or conceivably an even larger territory.

Nonetheless, the authors of this essay are in substantial agreement with Mathews and Justeson concerning the role of Emblem Glyphs as references to large political units. Even so, recent studies have left open one key question: if at least some Emblem Glyph main signs refer to polities (i.e., to the units over which Classic period rulers exercised real or imagined dominion), do other hieroglyphs refer to geographically specific places

*within* those polities? Where, in other words, are the place glyphs in Maya inscriptions? In the following section, we posit a category of glyphs that is related to but largely distinct from Emblem Glyphs. These signs apparently name specific sites and are comparable to the place glyphs long known from Central Mexican and other Mesoamerican cultures.

## The Place Name "Formula"

The most basic hieroglyphic sentences are usually divided into two parts, a verb and a subject. In the monumental inscriptions, the subject often takes the form of an individual's name along with a string of titles and epithets. Emblem Glyphs simply represent a title ("the holy [or divine] lord of . . .") that is usually placed after a noble's personal name. Such sentences may relate a historical or mythic event, and at times a second sentence may follow directly after the name and whatever titles accompany it. We propose that the function of this appended sentence or phrase is to specify the location of the event described in the preceding glyphs. In Figure 5 we illustrate a typical example of such an appended locative sentence (indicated by the arrow), after a longer passage that notes a Period Ending rite by Ruler 4 of Dos Pilas (Houston and Mathews 1985).

The internal structure of the appended sentence is illustrated in Figure 6. Although examples of the sequence show some variation in form, most have three parts in common. The first glyph is

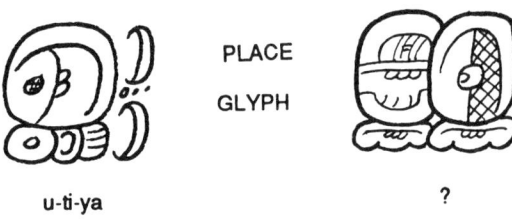

u-ti-ya      PLACE GLYPH      ?

Fig. 6 The place name "formula."

Fig. 5 Place name in sentence, recorded on Aguateca Stela 1: D1–D10 (I. Graham 1967: fig. 3).

traditionally known as the "Anterior Date Indicator" (or ADI, after Thompson 1950: 163). The ADI often occurs in connection with calendrical phrases such as Distance Numbers, where it is tied to the earlier of two joined dates. David Stuart (1990) has presented evidence that the ADI and its counterpart, the "Posterior Date Indicator," both record the Cholan verb root *ut,* "to happen, come to pass." Specifically, the ADI glyph consists of three syllables **u-ti-ya** for the completive verb *ut-i,* "it happened." When associated with Distance Numbers, dates function as the subjects of this verb. In the case of our appended expression the *ut-i* seems to function in a purely noncalendrical context. We should note that the form of the **u-ti-ya** compound seems to vary considerably, especially with the common replacement of the "muluc" sign (shown in Fig. 6) by the so-called xoc fish head. Both signs are functionally identical as phonetic **u** (Stuart 1990).

The second element of this "formula" is variable. In the examples under consideration, the glyphs that follow *ut-i* vary according to the sites where they occur. This pattern is just as consistent as the distribution noticed by Berlin in regard to Emblem Glyphs and by Stephen Houston (1986) for their functionally similar counterparts. We suggest that these variable glyphs specify locations. Moreover, several of these glyphs can be read phonetically, thus confirming their function as place names.

The locational function of the formula is particularly clear on the tablet of Temple 14 at Palenque, Mexico. Here, at the end of a short passage inscribed near two figures, the *ut-i* glyph precedes the glyph for "north," perhaps read pho-

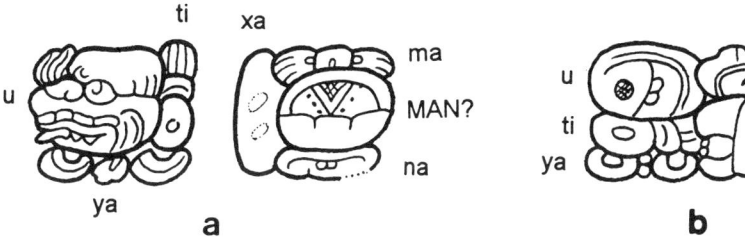

Fig. 7 *Xaman* and *Yaxha'* as place names

(a) Temple 14, Palenque: F4–G4, with *xaman* spelling (after Schele 1988: fig. 10.4)

(b) Dos Pilas Hieroglyphic Stairway 2: D6, east, with *Yaxha'* spelling (after unpublished drawing by Ian Graham).

netically as *xaman* (Fig. 7a; Closs 1988). We interpret this as a clear indication that the mythological action described and presumably depicted in the scene of the tablet "happened in the north."

In another example, on Dos Pilas Hieroglyphic Stairway 2, east, at D6b (Fig. 7b), the variable element after *ut-i* is spelled **YAX-a** for *Yaxha'*, "green water" or "clear water." We have already seen this place name in connection with the actual site of Yaxha, but in this example it is possibly a reference to another place or body of water, such as nearby Lake Petexbatun. The larger context of this location reference is not well understood, but "Yaxha" may have been the scene of some war-related event described in the sentence preceding the *ut-i* verb.

A third example of the *ut-i* formula (Figs. 8a–c) requires more detailed explanation. Twice in the inscriptions of Aguateca, *ut-i* precedes a glyph that doubtless served as the place name for the site (Fig. 8c). This glyph consists of the so-called *mahk'ina* prefix (Lounsbury 1974), which we believe should always be read *k'inich,* "sun-faced," followed by the logograph for *wits,* "hill, mountain" (Stuart 1987b).[1] The *wits* sign at Aguateca differs from other examples by the distinctive cleft at its top. The site's natural setting may explain the form of this glyph. Aguateca lies on the summit of an escarpment facing east, from which it receives the full morning sun across the swamps below. A natural fissure with a maximum depth of 50 m runs through the center of

[1] Floyd Lounsbury's (1974) *mahk'ina* reading has gained virtually complete acceptance in epigraphic circles, although we feel it now should be discarded in favor of the value *k'inich.* This honorific title, meaning "sun-eyed" or "sun-faced," is strongly suggested by several lines of evidence. In analyzing many of the graphic variants of this title, we find that they can be grouped into three principal forms: (a) the "affix" form that is, perhaps, most common; (b) the "head variant" representing the solar deity, with the affix form often attached to its backside; and (c) the so-called west glyph (Mathews n.d.a.), where the **chi** hand is combined in various ways with **K'IN** and **ni.** On occasion these forms may be combined to spell the title in question.

Lounsbury arrived at the *mahk'ina* value solely on the basis of the affix form. Looking at examples from the Late Classic

inscriptions (particularly those of Palenque, where Lounsbury concentrated his work), we can see how he arrived at this reading. The **ma** sign (T74) is usually present before the grouping of **K'IN** and **na,** where the latter "flanks" the **K'IN.** Lounsbury based his reading on the use of *mah* as an honorific term used in highland languages and Chol, and *q'inom,* "rich," and its cognate forms in Quiche, Cakchiquel, and Mam. Recently, Lyle Campbell (n.d.) has argued that these highland glosses probably have little to do with the glyphic title found in lowland inscriptions. We agree with his criticisms and point to further epigraphic evidence that cast doubt on this long-accepted reading.

In early examples of the affix form, **K'IN** is customarily absent. In its place we find the supposed "mirror" motif, presumably indicating a shiny or resplendent quality. The earliest

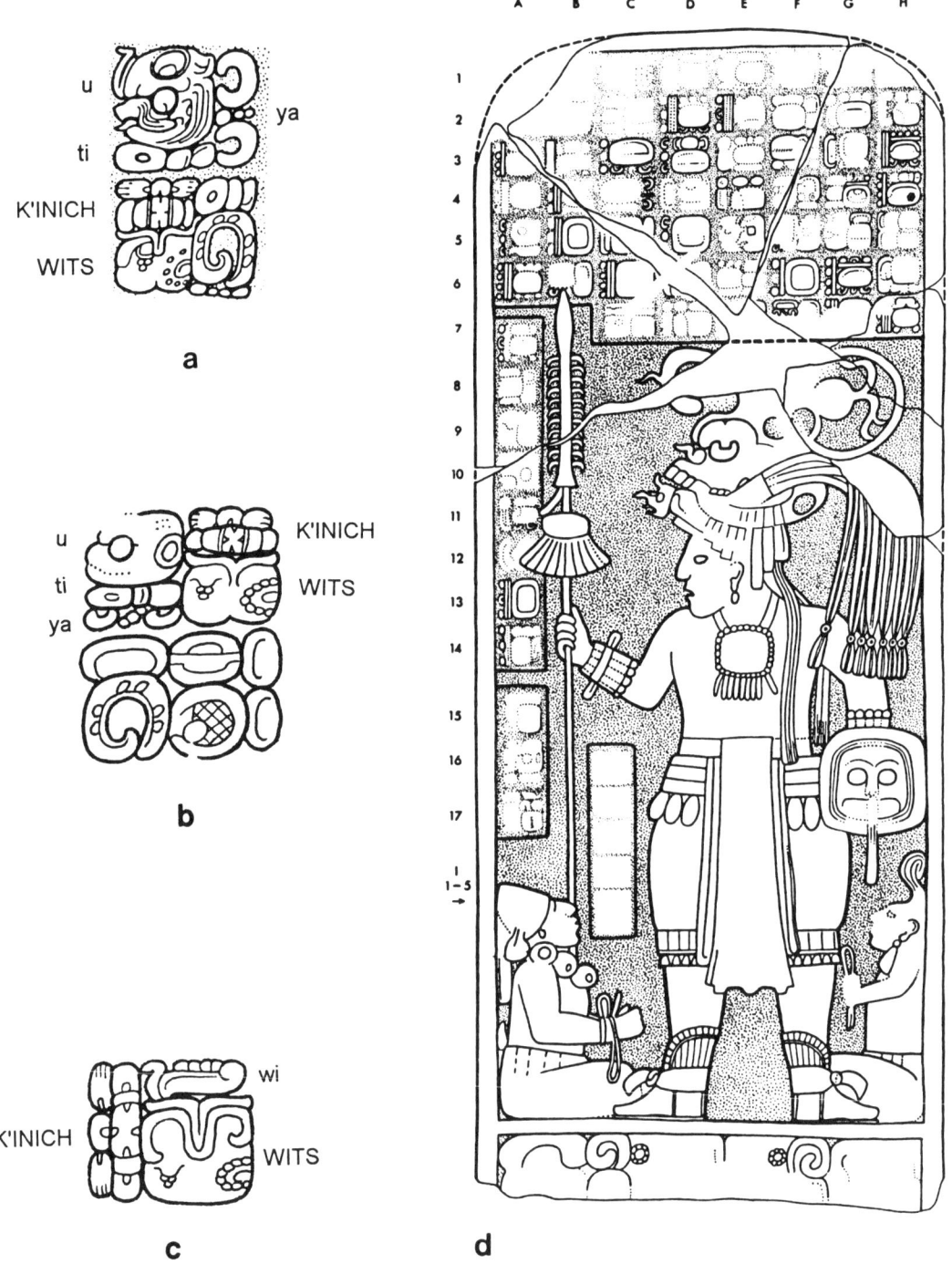

Fig. 8 Aguateca place names

(a) Aguateca Stela 1: D9–D10 (after I. Graham 1967: fig. 3)

(b) Aguateca Stela 2: G6–G7 (after I. Graham 1967: fig. 5)

(c) Aguateca Stela 7: F2 (after I. Graham 1967: fig. 17)

(d) Aguateca Stela 6 (after I. Graham 1967: fig. 15).

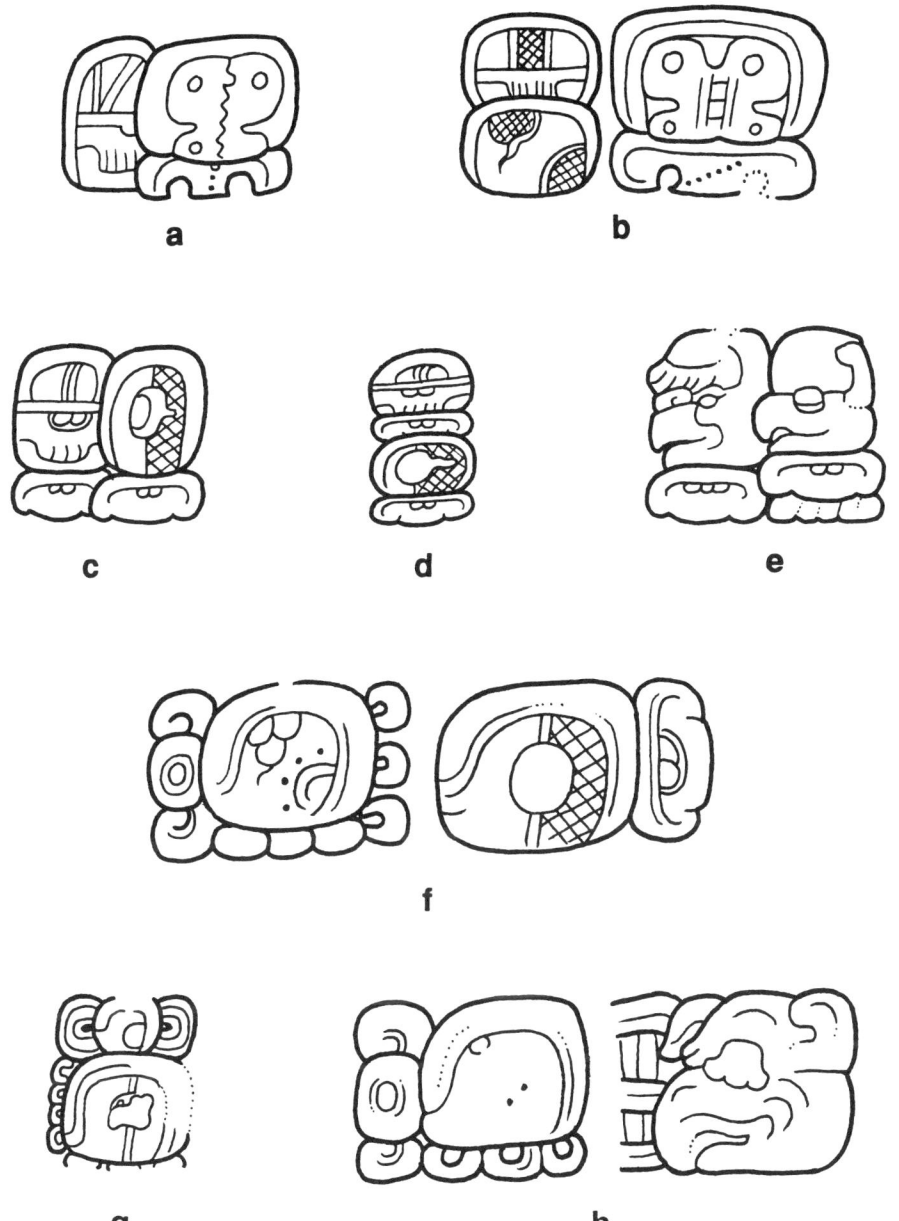

Fig. 9 Variants of the "sky-bone" compound

(a) Tikal Stela 31: G6 (after Jones and Satterthwaite 1982: fig. 52)

(b) Tikal 31: E27b–F27 (after Jones and Sattherthwaite 1982: fig. 52)

(c) Tablet of the Foliated Cross: L15 (after Lounsbury 1980: fig. 2)

(d) Alfarda, Temple of the Foliated Cross: L2b (after Lounsbury 1980: fig. 5)

(e) Copan Temple 11, Reviewing Stand: A'1 (after unpublished drawing by Barbara Fash, courtesy of Copan Mosaics Project)

(f) Dos Pilas Hieroglyphic Stairway 4, Step 3: H2–I1 (after drawing by Stephen Houston)

(g) El Peru Stela 30: pA3 (after drawing by Peter Mathews in Mayer 1989: pl. 183)

(h) Dos Pilas Hieroglyphic Stairway 4, Step 4: N1–M2 (after drawing by Stephen Houston).

the site (Graham 1967: 3). Aguateca, then, was named *K'inich (Cleft) Wits*—literally a "cleft and sun-faced hill." Moreover, Aguateca Stela 6 depicts a lord standing on a cleft hill sign, or "split hill" (Fig. 8d). We therefore believe this glyph to be a place name in the most literal sense. It is important to emphasize that this is *not* an Emblem Glyph, for Aguateca consistently uses the Emblem of Tikal and Dos Pilas as a title for its rulers (Houston and Mathews 1985). When we find this Aguateca place name after *ut-i,* it specifies that the event "happened at Sun-faced Split Hill."

*Ut-i* and the place glyph are the most basic parts of the formula under discussion, but they are not its only constituents. Often a third component we call the "sky-bone" glyph follows the place name (Figs. 9a–f). Also, it follows directional glyphs, locations in themselves, in sentences describing the so-called 819-day count ritual (Kelley 1976: fig. 17). The first sign of this glyph is usually the "sky" logograph, *kaan* or *chaan,* but this can be readily replaced by its head variant representing a bird. In many examples the phonetic complement **na** attaches to either of these variants. After *kaan* is another sign of highly variable form—T571, T598, or T599—also with **na.** These variants probably represent the forms of one sign as it changed through time, and the "bone" representation can be seen particularly in the early examples.[2] Its own head variant sign is also a bird, perhaps an owl, having a distinctive

trilobed element at the eye. This particular sign substitution occurs outside the context of the sky-bone glyph, as, for instance, part of the name of a ruler from Calakmul (Figs. 9g–h). With these inevitable substitutions and stylistic variations, the sky-bone compound may take several forms (Fig. 9). The meaning of the sky-bone glyph remains unknown, but its association with locational glyphs is apparent in inscriptions as well as iconographic contexts (see Chap. 4).

A related glyph is what we call "earth-bone," which appears in many contexts in the Dresden Codex (Fig. 10a). Here the sky sign is replaced by its conceptual opposite, *kab,* "earth." This never appears in the place name formula we describe, but the contexts of its occurrence suggest a locational association as well. In the third frame of Dresden page 38b, we find Chaak standing atop the earth-bone combination (their order curiously switched) with the caption above specifying earth-bone as the location of the act (Fig. 10b). The glyph even takes the locative prefix *ti,* and in every respect this structure parallels the frames on pages 65b–69b, discussed at the beginning of the chapter. The earth-bone compound also appears in the Classic inscriptions, although its locational significance is obscure (Fig. 10c).

Being the constant element in these glyphs, the "bone" sign deserves special consideration. Unfortunately, its phonetic value remains mysterious, although the final **na** complement should provide an important clue in any future efforts toward

---

"mirror" variants seem most similar to representations of bar pectorals worn across the chests of Maya rulers. The **na** signs are probably to be taken as constituents of this element, because their odd flanking positions indicate that they are not meant to be read as discrete glyphs. The **ma** prefix is optional, and because it appears as a part of the syllable **tsa,** probably has a more representational (rather than phonetic) role in this title.

If we take the *mahkina* affix in its many variants as a discrete sign that lacks any internal phonetic structure (at least in its pristine early examples), there remains little support for the **ma-K'IN-na** reading. The so-called west variant, however, provides the clue with which to arrive at a more satisfactory decipherment. As noted, this variant of the title in question is made up of three elements: **chi, k'in,** and **ni.** Often the **k'in** is infixed into the **chi** hand. In all respects it looks identical to glyphs for "west" in the Postclassic codices (**chi-K'IN-ni** for *chik'in,* "west"). But we must remember that infixation in

Maya writing leaves no clue as to reading order of the combined elements. In some cases, we find the title fully written with the three separate signs in the order **K'IN-ni-chi,** leading us to believe that it does not pertain to "west." The resulting *k'inich* is a well-known term in historical documents, best known perhaps in *K'inich Ahaw,* the common name of the sun god. Literally, this translates as "Sun-faced Lord." In our opinion, the title in question is based upon identification of some Maya rulers with the solar deity. This would explain the use of *k'inich* in personal names, not to mention the common head variant glyph representing the sun god himself.

[2] Although representing a bone of some sort, this sign is not to be confused with the longbone sign T510 that clearly reads **BAK,** "bone" (Stuart 1985a).

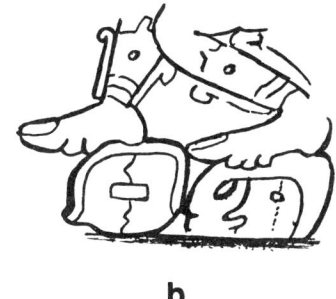
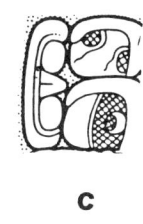

**a**

**b**

**c**

Fig. 10 The "earth-bone" expression

(a) "earth-bone" sign, Dresden 38b (Villacorta and Villacorta 1930: 86)

(b) Dresden 38b (Villacorta and Villacorta 1930: 86)

(c) Yaxchilan Lintel 25: VI (*CMHI* 3: 56).

decipherment. In some circumstances the sign may appear without sky or earth, and in these cases it alone seems to carry a strong locational significance. This can best be seen in hieroglyphic passages that make use of the so-called shell-star verb (Fig. 11) that refers to belligerent activity between sites (Riese 1984). As Peter Mathews (1991) notes, Emblem Glyph main signs often appear with this verb, apparently in reference to the polity that is attacked or victimized in some manner. In several texts, the bone, or (more commonly) its owl-head variant, follows directly after this verb, prefixed by the third person possessive pronoun *u,* "his, her, its." This is, in turn, followed by a personal name. Given the grammatical structure, we should expect the bone sign to somehow link the Emblem with the personal name and that the bone should refer to the Emblem (. . . the "X" of . . .). We might speculate that it specifies the location as being the "place" of the named individual, the victim of war. Clearly, in any case, the bone sign has suggestive locational associations.

To summarize, the formula contains three elements: the verb *ut-i,* a specified location, and, on occasion, the "sky-bone." At present, we translate this phrase: "It happened (at) [the location] . . ."—an expression indicating the setting of an event described in a preceding sentence.

However, we have yet to address a vexing grammatical issue that may call into question our interpretation of the *ut-i* formula. Where in our formula is the locative preposition ("in, at," etc.) that should occur after the verb and before the toponym? Prepositions are very common in the script (Mathews and Justeson 1984), and we know that Mayan languages would require a locative in the *ut-i* phrase as we have described it. Note, for example, that in the Books of Chilam Balam the preposition *t-,* "in, at" (contracted form), follows the verb *uch* (Yucatec cognate of Cholan *ut*) in both temporal and locative expressions that parallel the proposed reading of the hieroglyphic phrase (Victoria Bricker, personal communication, 1991): *uch-an t-u-ts'ok u-kuch k'atun,* "it happened at the end of the burden of the k'atun" (Tizimin p. 13, l. 10); *ti uch-an t-u-chi k'ak'nab,* "it happened there at the seashore" (Pérez p. 113, l. 4).

We should first note that locative preposition signs (most notably *ti*) sometimes do occur in the *ut-i* formula, as part of the place glyph. However, this does not necessarily address our question, inasmuch as Maya place names often begin with *Ti-* or *Ta-* (e.g., *Tiho',* the ancient name of Merida, or *Taitza,* which later came to be corrupted as Tayasal).

An explanation of this apparent discrepancy should not be based solely on considerations of Mayan grammar but should take into account certain features of the writing system as it relates to the spoken word. Through numerous examples it can be shown that the Maya script sometimes chooses *not* to represent certain grammatical parti-

a

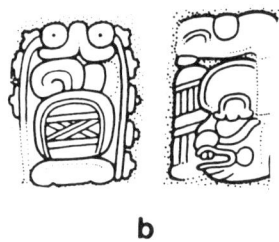

b

Fig. 11 The "Bone" sign as a reference to "place":

(a) Tonina Monument 122 (after unpublished drawing by Ian Graham)

(b) Naranjo, Hieroglyphic Stairway 1, Step 6 (I. Graham 1978: 109).

cles. For example, the plural ending -*ob* is apparently not indicated in phonetic spellings, and surely would be identified by now had it commonly been written. Other particles appear to be purely optional, such as the numerical classifier *te'*, which is required in speech but appears only occasionally between numerical coefficients and period or month glyphs (Figs. 12a–b).

Granted, written forms are difficult to compare with spoken ones, which remain, despite the best efforts of historical linguists, very poorly understood. Nonetheless, evidence does exist to suggest that Maya glyphs represent an imperfect reflection of speech. In the case of the numerical

classifier *te'*, we find it to be included in all the dates recorded (in the Latin script) from the Books of Chilam Balam, where it is interposed between the coefficient and month name, as in *t-u 11 te' Xul*, "on the eleventh day of Xul." As Hermann Beyer (1937) and J. Eric S. Thompson (1937) noted many decades ago, precisely the same structure exists in the inscriptions of northern Yucatan, with the *te'* sign in its proper position. However, numerous cases also occur where the required *te'* sign disappears from the grouping of elements. We are left to conclude that *te'* is purely optional as a written element, and, when absent, was supplied by the reader.

a

b

Fig. 12 Comparison showing optionality of *te'* (indicated by arrow)

(a) Yaxchilan, Lintel 1: A2 (*CMHI* 2: 13)

(b) Yaxchilan Stela 11: D3 (after Thompson 1950: fig. 56).

**a**                                          **b**

Fig. 13 Optionality of *tu* (indicated by arrow) in texts from Chichen Itza

(a) Temple of the Four Lintels, 4: A1–B2
(Beyer 1937: fig. 641)

(b) Temple of the Four Lintels, 1: A1–A2
(Beyer 1937: fig. 639).

Similarly, and more pertinent to our argument, locative prepositions can be shown to be optional elements in the writing system. Returning to the hieroglyphic dates of northern Yucatan, we note that many, but not all, month notations take the *tu* prefix, corresponding to the preposition *t-* combined with the possessive pronoun *u*, as in the example given above, *t-u 11 te' Xul*, "on the eleventh day of Xul." At Chichen Itza, for example, the date 9 Lamat 11 Yax is rendered in one text *9 Lamat k'in tu 11 Yax*, and in another *9 Lamat k'in 11 Yax* (Figs. 13a–b). The *tu* sign, including the preposition, is completely optional. The same feature is more simply demonstrated by comparing two dates recorded on the Early Classic hieroglyphic lintels from Structure 12 at Yaxchilan (Figs. 14a–b). The contexts of these two dates are identical: both follow the same passages and are themselves associated with identical verbs. In one, the preposition *ta* is clearly given before the day sign 1 Cimi ("on 1 Cimi . . ."); in the other, the date is presented without any prepositional prefix. In such instances, we believe that the available space around the numerical coefficient conditions the presence of the locative. Where the coefficient is small, as in "1 Cimi," the *ta* is easily included as "filler." A similar comparison of two structurally identical dates from Tortuguero Monument 6 shows the same principle at work (Figs. 14c–d).

Prepositions would seem to be optional in noncalendrical contexts as well. The so-called af-

fix cluster that accompanies seating and accession verbs to designate an office or position (H. Berlin 1968: 147; Mathews and Justeson 1984) usually takes the preposition *ti* or *ta* (reading something like ". . . in the rulership," for example). Although Mathews and Justeson feel that the locative is a necessary component, we cite one example from Copan where no such preposition exists. The accession verb is simply followed by *ahaw*, "lord," rather than the customary *ta ahaw-lel* (Fig. 15).

Finally, in the Dresden Codex we see examples where locative prepositions are freely dropped from place glyphs. The earth-bone combination, discussed above as a probable locational reference, is a consistent part of the hieroglyphic captions on pages 32b–35b (Figs. 16a–d). In two of four parallel passages we find the earth-bone with the preposition *ta*, whereas in the remaining two cases it is absent. This pattern cannot be explained by different grammatical constructions, but rather by the whim of the scribe.

Our lengthy discussion of preposition signs shows that they are not always a necessity in hieroglyphic spelling. Why are prepositions and other grammatical elements, such as numerical classifiers and plural endings, optional in the script or altogether absent? The answer may be found in the tricky and largely unresolved issues of historical linguistics and the mechanics of the writing system. As a logo-syllabic script, Maya writing may be an imprecise reflection of speech. This can be

15

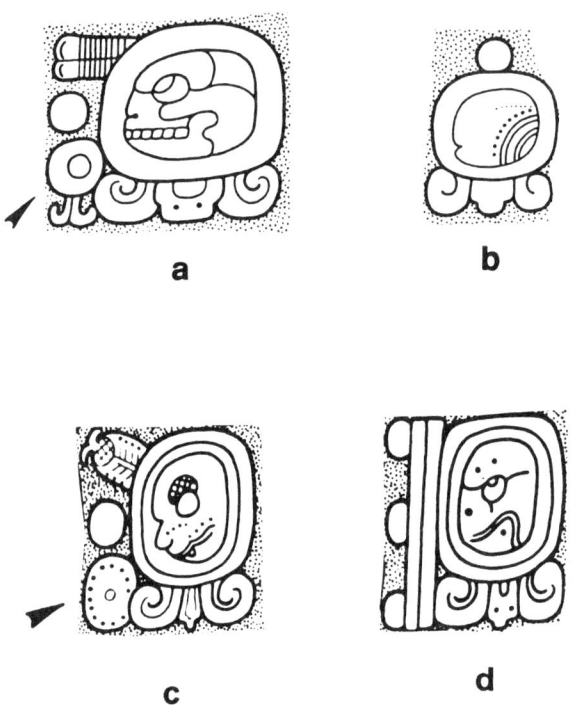

a   b

c   d

Fig. 14 Optionality of *ta* (indicated by arrow) at Yaxchilan and Tortuguero

(a) Yaxchilan Lintel 35: C4 (*CMHI* 3: 79)
(b) Yaxchilan Lintel 37: C6a (*CMHI* 3: 83)
(c) Tortuguero Monument 6: B6 (drawing courtesy of Ian Graham, Peabody Museum, Harvard University)

(d) Tortuguero Monument 6: B11 (drawing courtesy of Ian Graham, Peabody Museum, Harvard University).

Fig. 15 Optionality of *ti/ta* in the affix cluster. Copan Temple 11, Bench.

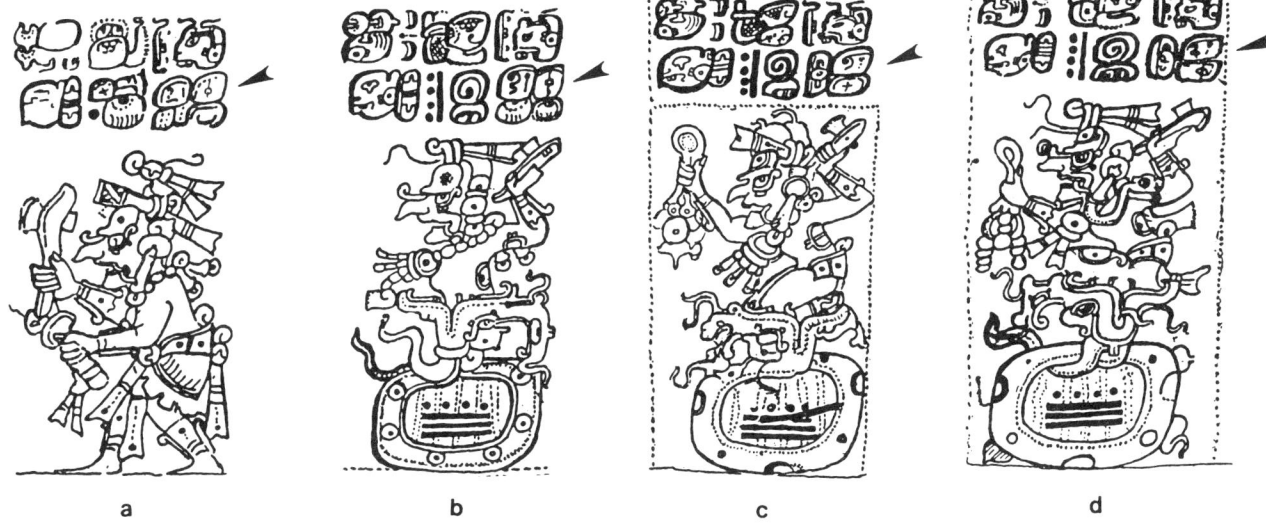

|     |     |     |     |
| --- | --- | --- | --- |
| a   | b   | c   | d   |

Fig. 16 Optionality of *ti* in the Dresden Codex

(a) Dresden 32b (Villacorta and Villacorta 1930: fig. 74)

(b) Dresden 33b (Villacorta and Villacorta 1930: fig. 76)

(c) Dresden 34b (Villacorta and Villacorta 1930: fig. 78)

(d) Dresden 35b (Villacorta and Villacorta 1930: fig. 80).

best shown, perhaps, by a short inscription of three glyphs from Copan, Honduras (Fig. 17). The first glyph presents the very abbreviated date "3 Lamat," followed by a dedication verb (perhaps based on the root *wa,* "to raise") that carries none of its customary verbal affixes. The final glyph refers to the inscribed object, a stone vessel that is called a *saklaktun* ("artificial stone vessel"), also without the usual possessive pronoun. The three glyphs represent the three basic components of Maya hieroglyphic sentences—a date, a verb, and a subject—but they are completely stripped of the necessary grammatical affixation. Possibly the more "obvious" grammatical particles, like classifiers and plural endings, were provided by readers in the context of oral presentations or performances. This interactive aspect of Maya inscriptions deserves much more study and has recently been addressed in other areas of Mesoamerica (Monaghan 1990). However, the oral dimensions

of ancient scripts have been long realized in Old World studies. In archaic Sumerian, for example, the reader routinely supplied a great deal of the grammatical and lexical information when reading tablets that were essentially mnemonic in character (Civil and Biggs 1966; Civil 1976).

Yet, admittedly, we hesitate to cite the "imperfections" of the Maya writing system to account for the general absence of locative prepositions with place glyphs—any explanation that posits omissions (or original "error") instead of unclear understandings on our part is bound to raise suspicions. However, we would point out that all writing systems are to one degree or another incomplete records of speech. Specialists in Sumerian cuneiform (a logo-syllabic writing system that is typologically similar to that of the Maya), commonly acknowledge the scribal underrepresentation of sounds that "should" be there (Diakonoff 1976: 101–102; Michalowski 1991). As Diakonoff

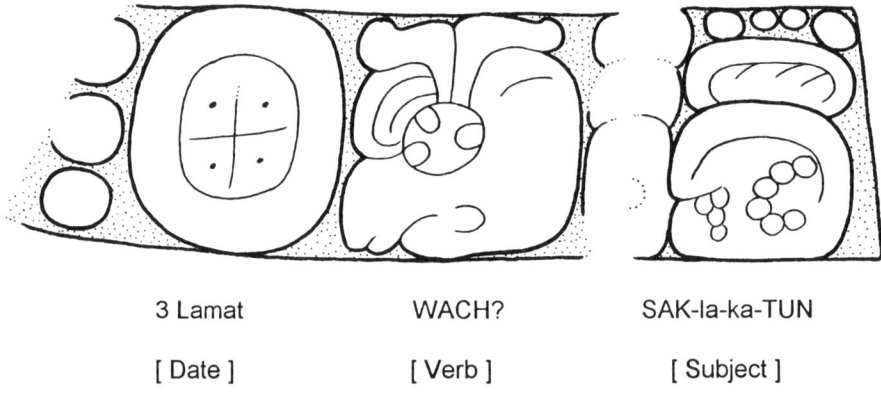

| 3 Lamat | WACH? | SAK-la-ka-TUN |
| [ Date ] | [ Verb ] | [ Subject ] |

Fig. 17 Text from a Copan *incensario,* CPN 260 and 277 (drawing by David Stuart, courtesy of William Fash, director, Copan Mosaics Project).

(1976: 109) puts it, "there was nothing that could prevent a scribe from omitting a sign which he thought superfluous." Maya scribes may have viewed locative prepositions as superfluous elements when attached to locational glyphs. Whatever the case, we are hopeful that future investigations will confirm or disprove our arguments about the occasional omission of some signs in the Maya script. In the meantime, these points of detail do not detract from much of the evidence that place glyphs can be identified in the Classic inscriptions.

# CHAPTER 2

# A Working List of Maya Place Glyphs

Because the place name formula described in the previous chapter is relatively common in Maya inscriptions, we can readily identify many place glyphs and, when decipherable, the actual place names of well-known sites of the Classic period. For the most part these place glyphs are distinct from Emblem Glyphs, although there are some exceptions discussed below.

## Dos Pilas

One of the clearest place glyphs appears in the texts of Dos Pilas, Guatemala (Figs. 18a–b). The glyph in question includes the "darkened *imix*" logograph for *ha'*, "water," below a rather unusual sign representing a serpent with vegetal "wings." In most instances, this combination follows *ut-i* (Figs. 18b–c). Similar to the Aguateca "split hill" sign, it can also appear on Dos Pilas monuments beneath the feet of standing lords, in basal registers separating rulers from crouching captives. Clear examples of this locational imagery occur on Dos Pilas Stelae 2 and 5 (Fig. 18d).

The place glyph interpretation helps elucidate several previously obscure passages in hieroglyphic texts. For instance, the engraved bone designated Miscellaneous Text 28 (MT-28) from Tikal Burial 116 (Fig. 18e) mentions the death date of Dos Pilas Ruler 2 (Houston and Mathews 1985: 15; Proskouriakoff 1973: 170). It has been noted elsewhere that Dos Pilas shared its Emblem Glyph with Tikal (Houston and Mathews 1985: 6–7). Yet, on MT-28, Ruler 2's name does not appear with the Emblem, but rather with the Dos

Pilas place glyph, accompanied by the male agentive prefix *ah,* "he of . . ." (here in the form of T229). This title of origin distinguishes Ruler 2, "He of Dos Pilas," from the local Tikal lords in a way that the Emblem Glyph would not (similar titles of origin will be treated in more detail below). If our interpretation is correct, the Dos Pilas glyph allows us to differentiate references to particular sites of the Petexbatun region, such as Dos Pilas and Aguateca, that at one time fell within a single political domain.

As noted, the Dos Pilas place glyph employs the "darkened *imix*" sign as its second and last component. This sign, following Fox and Justeson (1984), is very probably a logograph for *ha'*, "water." Such usage recalls modern Mayan toponyms, which commonly end in *ha'* (as in Yaxha'). Others suggest that the darkened imix is **NAB,** "lake, pool, general body of water" (Linda Schele, personal communication, 1989), but we prefer the Fox and Justeson reading. *Nab* is already firmly attested in the script, in the form of an iconic sign showing the root and blossom of the water lily, *naab* in Yucatec Maya (see Fig. 29). In addition, in at least one place the glyph for "atole," *sak ha',* includes the *imix* sign (Fig. 19). Thus, the reading of **HA** is, in our judgment, more secure than alternative decipherments.

## Altar de Sacrificios

Stephen D. Houston (1986) has recently associated a certain sign combination with Altar de Sacrificios. We now believe that this glyph falls

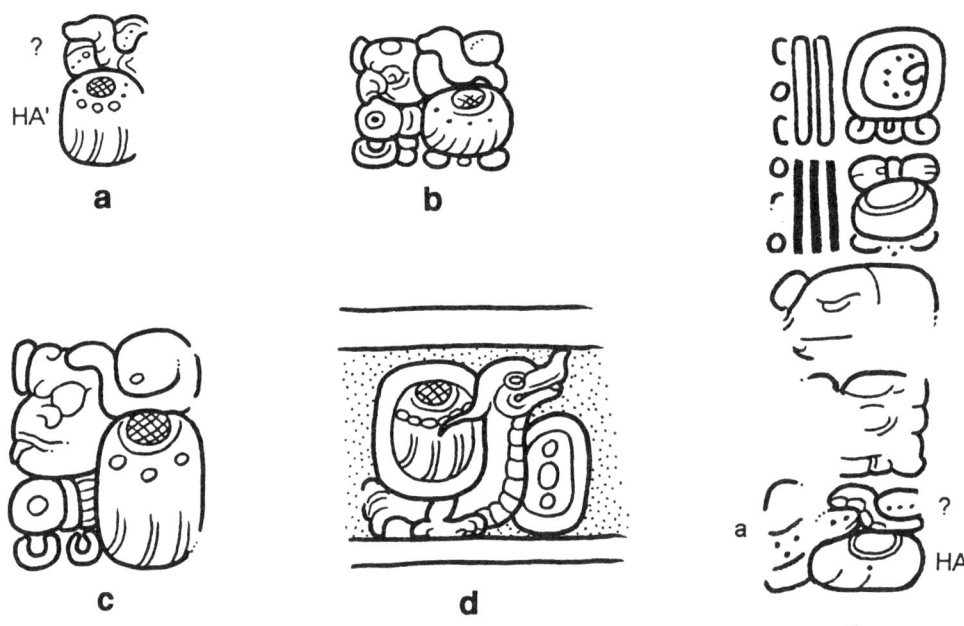

Fig. 18 Dos Pilas place name

(a) Dos Pilas Stela 8: H15a (after drawing by Ian Graham)

(b) Dos Pilas Stela 14: G2 (after drawing by Stephen Houston)

(c) Dos Pilas place name after *ut-i* expression, Dos Pilas Stela 15: F6 (after drawing by Stephen Houston)

(d) basal register of Dos Pilas Stela 2 (drawing by David Stuart)

(e) MT-28 text from Burial 116, Tikal (after drawing courtesy of Christopher Jones, Tikal Project, University Museum, University of Pennsylvania).

into our category of place glyphs. On Altar de Sacrificios Stela 18, J10–J11, it follows *ut-i* and precedes the "sky compound" (Fig. 20b). Another example of the glyph takes the *ah-* agentive prefix (Fig. 20c), in the same fashion as the "he of Dos Pilas" glyph on the Tikal bone. In other texts, the Altar glyph is combined with *ahaw*, "lord," to form a title for nobles and rulers of the site (Fig. 20d).

## Ucanal

Another place name, probably referring to Ucanal and used as part of the Emblem Glyph of the site (Mathews n.d.b), appears on Naranjo Stela 32, at W4, and on Altar 12 from Caracol,

both times in association with the *ut-i* verb (Figs. 21a–b). Its three parts are read together as **K'AN WITS NAL,** or "yellow hill *nal*" (the *nal* suffix will be discussed momentarily). Several other examples of this glyph occur at Ucanal and in the inscriptions of nearby sites (Figs. 21c–d). *Wits,* "hill," as we have already demonstrated, forms part of the Aguateca place name ("Sun-faced Hill"), as well as of many other toponyms. David Stuart (1987b) has previously noted the place name *Hix wits,* "Jaguar Hill," in the texts of Yaxchilan and Piedras Negras.[3] The use of "hill" in many ancient Maya place names reflects the propensity of the Classic Maya to settle on high ground (Puleston 1983: 23).

[3] The site associated with the *Hix Wits* Emblem or place glyph has yet to be identified. The glyph's appearance at Yaxchilan, Piedras Negras, and Itsimte indicates that the site may lie in the vicinity of these three sites, perhaps in the

SAK HA'

Fig. 19 *Sakha'* in spelling from unprovenanced vessel of early Late Classic date (after Houston, Stuart, and Taube 1989: fig. 2).

The sign in the Ucanal place glyph we read as **NAL,** following Yurii Knorosov (1967), deserves further comment. Knorosov noted that *nal* means a young ear of maize in many Mayan languages, and his reading was based mainly on iconographic identifications of examples from the codices. However, more recent analysis of its usage in the Classic inscriptions confirms Knorosov's reading; among the clearest substitutions is one from the Uxmal (Fig. 22), which confirms on phonetic grounds the reading of **NAL.**

A second issue involves the proper place of the sign in the reading order of glyphs within a block of signs. In the Ucanal glyph, this vegetal element appears above the hill sign, where seemingly it should be read after **K'AN** and before **WITS.** T86, as it is labeled in J. Eric S. Thompson's catalogue (1962), is indeed almost always a "superfix," attached to the top of main signs. In many examples, however, it can be shown that this sign is simply an abbreviation of a larger discrete element of the script that at first glance seems to consist of two elements, a superfix and a main sign. We call such signs "compound signs." In its complete form, the lower portion below the common vegetal leaf represents a corncob, hence *nal.* This appears in only a few cases, however, for usually Maya scribes preferred to "overlay"

other signs atop the corncob, leaving the vegetal sign T86 peeking over the top. We know of many other signs that operate on the same graphic principle: the so-called *ah po* sign T186, for example, is but an abbreviation of T186: 513. Both are always read **AHAW,** and, as a superfix, the T186 abbreviation is always read after the main sign below it (see the earlier description of Emblem Glyphs). Similarly, the vegetal **NAL** sign is likely to be read after the main sign below it, producing the reading **K'AN WITS NAL** for the Ucanal glyph.

## Naranjo

The glyph illustrated in Figure 23 may have represented the original name of Naranjo, or of some nearby location. It has two spellings—T74: 508v: 74 and T502: 114.502—both of which read **ma-xa-ma,** or *maxam,* whose meaning remains unknown. The compound occurs twice at Naranjo after *ut-i,* so that its identification with the site is strong, but by no means certain. A painted vessel, probably from the Naranjo region (M. Coe 1973: 103), bears the glyph **A-ma-xa-ma,** or *ah maxam,* within the painter's signature (Fig. 23c). We have already seen the *ah-* agentive prefix with the place names of Dos Pilas and Altar de Sacrificios. On this vessel the glyph probably identifies the home site of the painter ("he of *maxam*").

Naranjo has three other place names in its inscriptions, but their affiliations are unclear. One appears on Stela 22 (H4), apparently naming the location where "Smoke Squirrel" of Naranjo captured "Smoke Frog" from Tikal (Fig. 24a). The chief elements of this place glyph are *k'an* and a rabbit's head. Another place name on Stela 23 is probably read *Sakha'* ("White Water"), which follows *ut-i* (G15–H15; Fig. 24b). This location, possibly the place of a battle, may correspond to the modern Lake Sacnab, directly adjacent to Lake

western Peten of present-day Guatemala. We should add that the **HIX** reading for the jaguar eye is attested on, among other sculptures, Dos Pilas Panel 19 and Hieroglyphic Stairway 3, which show the glyph preceded by a knot affix, read

by Justeson and Fox as **h-** (Justeson 1984) and by us as **hi** (the same affix helps spell a common hieroglyphic compound for "deer," **chi-h[i]**). Here, the affix serves as a phonetic complement: **(hi)-HIX.**

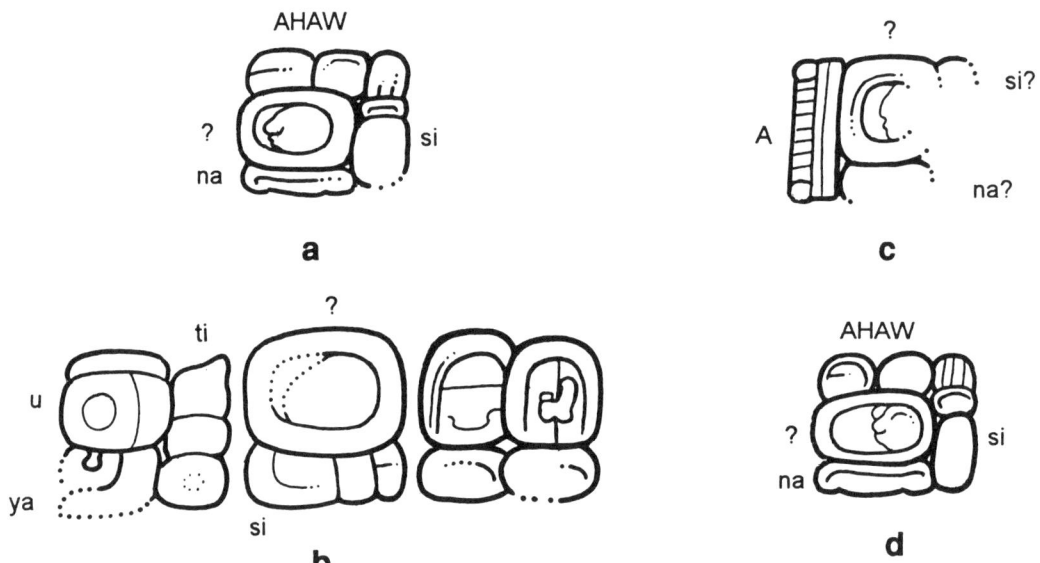

Fig. 20 Altar de Sacrificios place name

(a) Altar de Sacrificios Stela 5: C12, note *ahaw* title
    (after J. Graham 1972: fig. 14)
(b) Altar de Sacrificios Stela 18: J10–J11, with place
    name after *ut-i* compound (after J. Graham 1972:
    fig. 46)

(c) Altar de Sacrificios place name with *ah* prefix,
    recorded on Sculpted Panel 4: zDz6 (after J. Gra-
    ham 1972: fig. 59)
(d) Altar de Sacrificios place name with *ahaw* title, re-
    corded on Stela 4: C5 (after J. Graham 1972: fig. 12).

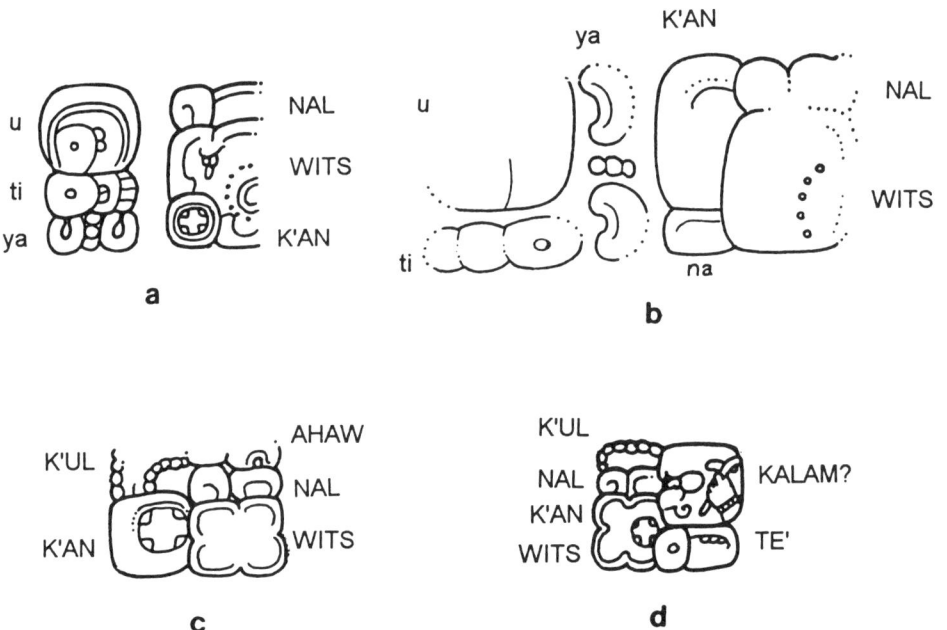

Fig. 21 Ucanal place name

(a) Naranjo Stela 32: X4–X5 (after *CMHI* 2: 86)
(b) Caracol Altar 12 (drawing by Stephen Houston)
(c) Ucanal place name in Emblem Glyph, Ucanal Stela
    E1 (after *CMHI* 2: 159)

(d) Ucanal place name in Emblem Glyph variant,
    Ucanal Stela 4: C3 (after *CMHI* 2: 159).

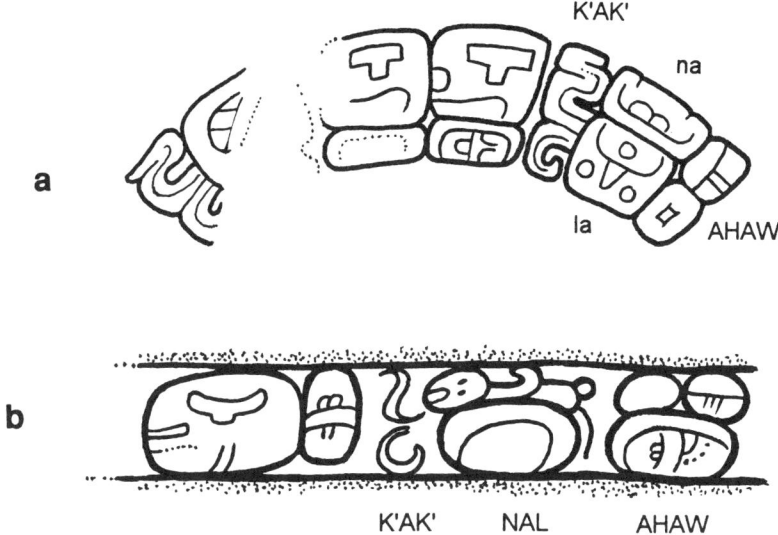

Fig. 22 *Nal* substitution from Uxmal ballcourt marker and capstone (drawings by David Stuart from the originals).

Yaxha (Linda Schele, personal communication, 1988). Stela 10 from Naranjo shows yet another place name, apparently the locale where the ruler "Shield God K" (not to be confused with Dos Pilas' Ruler 2 of the same name) was born on 9.17.0.2.12 in the Maya Long Count (Fig. 24c). Unfortunately, this place glyph cannot be firmly identified with any particular site or location.

## Copan

The inscriptions of Copan frequently contain the glyph illustrated in Figure 25, which may be transliterated as **OX-wi-ti-k(i),** or *Oxwitik,* again of unknown meaning ("Three *Witik*s"?).[4]

On the "mat inscription" of Stela J, this sign appears between *ut-i* and the "sky compound," clearly indicating its function as a place name (Fig. 25b). In all likelihood, *oxwitik* is the ancient name of Copan itself, or at least of part of the site or valley.

The Copan inscriptions also contain several references to named hills (Fig. 26). *Oxwits,* "Three Hills," is used on Stela J in the title *Oxwits Ahaw,* "Three Hills Lord," for K'inich Yax K'uk' Mo', the important Early Classic ruler of the site (Fig. 26a). It remains to be seen whether *Oxwits* is semantically or phonologically related to *Oxwitik.* Much more common are the references to two named hills: **MO-WITS,** or *Mo'wits* ("Macaw

[4] The meaning of the term spelled by **wi-ti-ki** remains a mystery, but the single occurrence of this term outside of the Copan inscriptions might eventually lead to a decipherment. On the well-known stirrup-handled cacao vessel excavated from Tomb 19 at Rio Azul (Hall et al., 1990; Stuart 1988b), two glyphs, C and D, read **TA-wi-ti-ki ka-ka-wa.** This is a prepositional phrase that refers to the contents of the vessel, roughly translatable as "for (the) *witik* cacao." Here, then, *witik* may refer to some added element in the cacao recipe, possibly a floral substance. Interestingly, plants are very common in Maya and Mesoamerican place names, and Copan's "Three *Witik*s" may refer directly to an unknown species of plant. So far, the search for *witik* among Maya botanical terms has been fruitless.

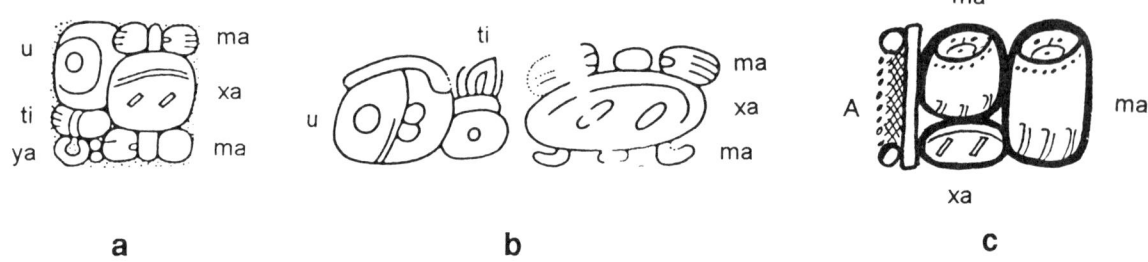

**a**        **b**        **c**

Fig. 23 Naranjo place name

(a) Naranjo Stela 8: B8 (*CMHI* 2: 27)
(b) probable example on Naranjo Altar 1: D7–D8
    (*CMHI* 2: 104)

(c) *ah maxam* on unprovenanced vessel, position A'
    (Coe 1973: 103).

**a**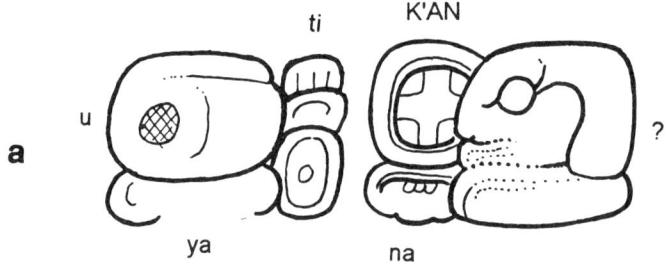

**b**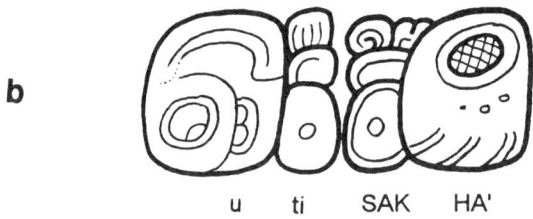

**c**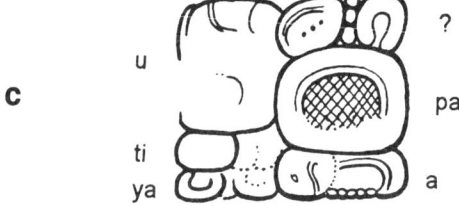

Fig. 24 Unusual place names at Naranjo

(a) "rabbit head" place name on Naranjo Stela 22: G4–
    H4 (*CMHI* 2: 56)
(b) *Sakha'* place name on Naranjo Stela 23: G15–H15
    (*CMHI* 2: 58)

(c) the location where Shield God K was born, on
    Naranjo Stela 10: B4 (*CMHI* 2: 31).

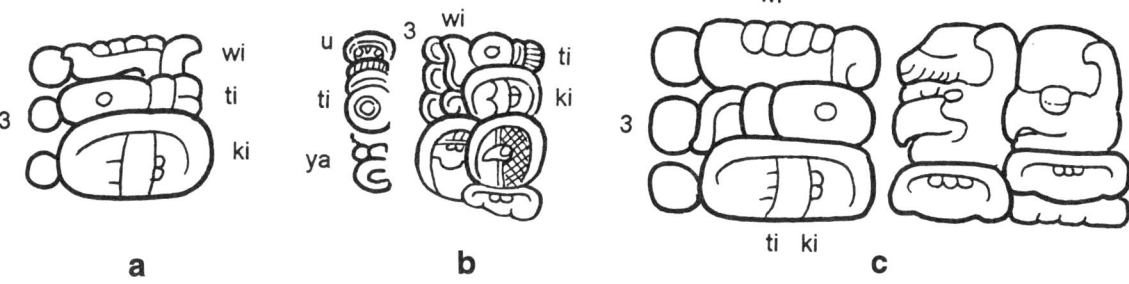

Fig. 25 Copan place name, *Oxwitik*

(a) Copan Altar Q: D5
(b) Copan Stela J: Block 36
(c) Copan Temple 11, Reviewing Stand: Z1'–A'1

(all drawings courtesy of William Fash, director, Copan Mosaics Project).

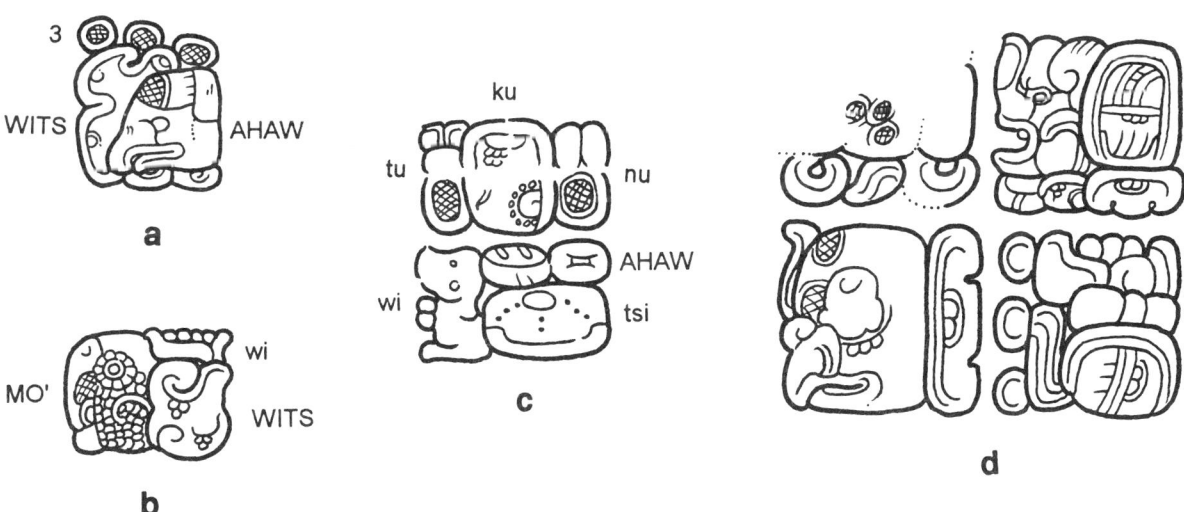

Fig. 26 Other place names at Copan

(a) *Oxwits,* Copan Stela J: block 22
(b) *Mo'wits,* Copan Stela B, back
(c) *Tukunwits,* Temple 11, west door, south panel: C2–C3

(d) Stela 10: C9–D10 (all drawings courtesy of William Fash, director, Copan Mosaics Project).

a                     b                     c

Fig. 27 Seibal place name

(a) Seibal Hieroglyphic Stairway 1, Panel 4, W2b–X1 (after unpublished drawing by Ian Graham)
(b) Seibal Stela 10: B11 (drawing by James Porter)

(c) the Seibal Emblem Glyph, Seibal Hieroglyphic Stairway 1, Panel 4: W1 (after unpublished drawing by Ian Graham).

Hill," Fig. 26b), and **tu-ku-nu(?)-WITS,** possibly for *Tukunwits,* the meaning of which is unknown (Fig. 26c).[5] Both names usually appear together, and perhaps in association with other place names that do not refer to mountains. We still do not completely understand the contexts of these references, nor are we sure if these identify actual hills (historical or mythical) or buildings (in the sense of artificial mountains; note the *wits* motifs on the exterior corners of Structure 10L–22) in Copan's acropolis. However, "Macaw Hill" is represented iconographically on Copan Stela B as the setting of the 18 Rabbit's Period Ending rite on 9.15.0.0.0. More detailed work with the relevant passages at Copan may eventually clarify some of these ambiguities.

In one example from Copan Stela 10, which dates to 9.11.0.0.0, the main sign of the Copan Emblem Glyph appears after a probable *ut-i* expression (Fig. 26d). Appearing with the sign are the sky compound and its companion glyph, now in head variant form, as well as the *Oxwitik* glyph. This clause raises two possibilities: that the Copan main sign is equivalent to the *Oxwitik* place name, or that it represents a region either greater or smaller than that specified by *Oxwitik.*

A similar pattern in which a general place name is juxtaposed with a more narrow reference occurs at Palenque (Fig. 32).

Structure 10L–22A (Fash et al. 1992), the probable *Popol Nah* or Council House in Copan's main acropolis, was decorated on its exterior with several large hieroglyphs that seem to be locations. Those that can be identified seem to be mythological in nature and will be treated in Chapter 5. However, it is worth noting here that these glyphs were probably placed below seated figures on the building's facade, rather like the Chaak figures in the Dresden Codex, as described at the beginning of Chapter 1.

## Seibal

In a few examples, the apparent place name of Seibal also follows *ut-i* (Fig. 27). Interestingly, it is much the same as the main sign of the local Emblem Glyph, the principal graphic distinction being the addition of T606: 23, **TAN-na,** or *tan,* "within," as a possible locative prefix, and subfix

---

[5] Nikolai Grube (personal communication, 1989) has suggested to one of the authors (D. Stuart) that *Tukunwits* may refer to another hill named for a bird. *Ukum* is a common term for "dove," and with the locative prefix *ti-,* the result

would be quite similar. However, there are no visual clues in the form of logographs to confirm the meaning "Dove Hill," and we must leave the matter open for the moment.

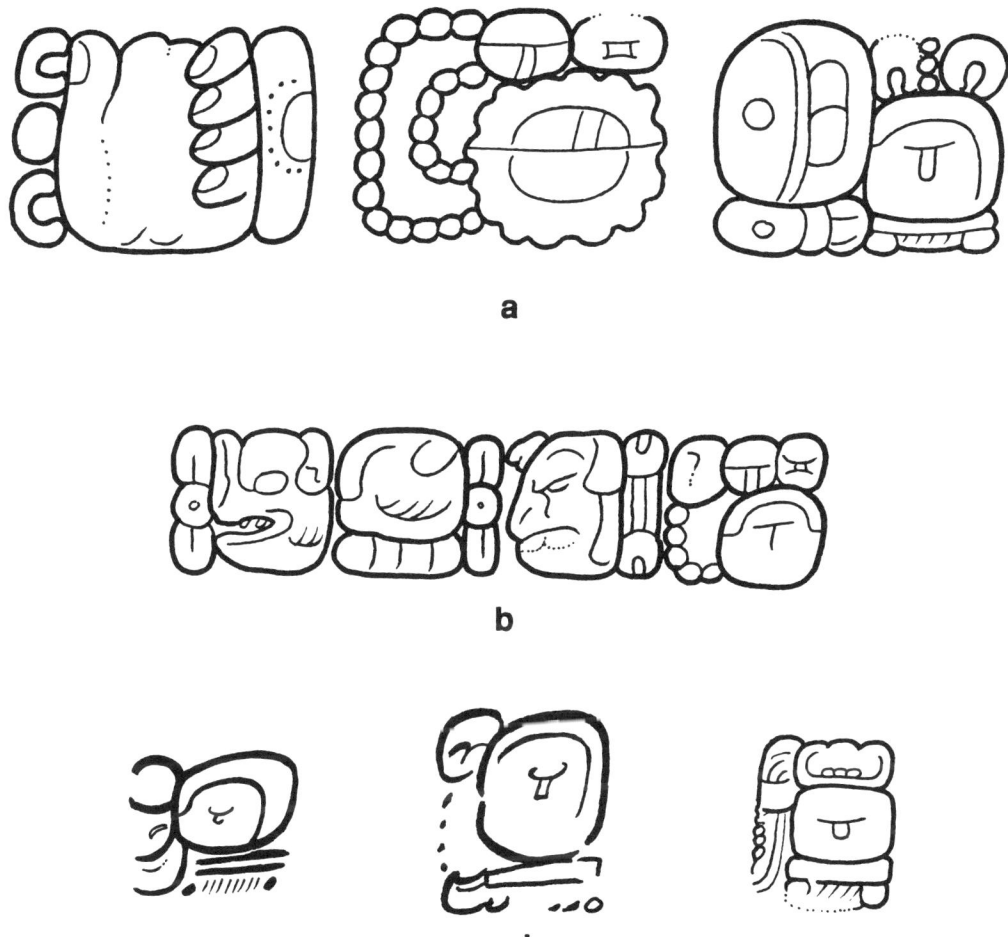

a

b

c          d          e

Fig. 28 Motul de San José

(a) Stela 1: A6–B7 (Maler 1910: pl. 45)
(b) sculptor's signature, showing "Ik-site" Emblem
    Glyph, Stela 1: C1–F1 (after unpublished draw-
    ing by Ian Graham)
(c) title of origin, unprovenanced vessel (Dumbarton
    Oaks photographic archive)

(d) title of origin, unprovenanced vessel (Kerr 1990:
    233)
(e) Yaxchilan Stela 21: pH8 (after Morley 1937–38, V:
    pl. 104b).

T173.[6] Despite their graphic similarity, there is a pronounced difference in function between this posited place name and the Seibal Emblem Glyph.

## Motul de San José

A possible place glyph occurs after *ut-i* on Stela 1 from Motul de San José (Fig. 28). The sign contains the *ik* main sign, which Joyce Marcus (1976: fig. 1.7) identifies as the Emblem Glyph of Motul de San José. However, her identification is uncertain, for a very different Emblem (with main sign T679v) occurs nearby in the inscription (Fig. 28a). Another problem stems from the fact that the probable Motul place glyph differs from Marcus' Motul Emblem: the *ik* sign appears above the glyph **A** or **a.** The same combination occurs in titles of origin (see below, this chapter; Figs. 28c–e). We suspect that the final element, much like the examples from Yaxha, carries the meaning of *ha',* "water." The one compound with a **na** glyph is probably a variant of the others, in this case with a more elaborate *ik* logograph.[7]

## Calakmul(?)

Another possible place name appears on an unprovenanced panel published by Linda Schele and Mary Ellen Miller (1986: pl. 101). Once again the place glyph follows *ut-i* at the end of an inscription. Its principal elements are **OX-TE-TUN-ni,** *Ox-te'tun,* "Three Stones" (Figs. 29a–b), and a second combination consisting of a superfix (T324) above a main sign formed from two conflated elements, a **chi** hand (T671) and **TUN** (T528), for

*tunich,* "of stone" (Fig. 29c). Substitution patterns in the inscriptions of Palenque show that the T324 superfix, which represents a water-lily pad and blossom, may be read *nab,* "lake, pool, body of water." Together, the signs probably provide the place name *Nabtunich,* "Stone Aguada(?)."[8]

Both the *Oxte'tun* and *Nabtunich* glyphs are closely connected with the so-called snake head Emblem Glyph found in inscriptions throughout the southern Maya lowlands. In one case, for example, a person named on Hieroglyphic Stairway 1 from Naranjo carries the "snake" Emblem and is later named *Ah Nabtunich,* "He of *Nabtunich*" (Fig. 30). Joyce Marcus (1976: 51) and Jeffrey Miller (1974) believed the snake Emblem to be that of Calakmul. Peter Mathews (personal communication, 1980), Linda Schele (1984a: 24), and others attribute the Emblem Glyph to El Peru, Guatemala, apparently because Ian Graham had demonstrated an El Peru provenance for a set of monuments formerly assigned to Calakmul (Graham 1988).

In our opinion, the evidence now favors the interpretation of Marcus and Miller.[9] For one, the snake Emblem appears at El Peru only in the names of foreigners. For another, texts from Calakmul show that *Oxte'tun* and *Nabtunich* appear in association with local events and with rulers who clearly use the snake Emblem (Ruppert and Denison 1943: figs. 50c, 51b). Furthermore, at Naachtun, a site approximately 30 km from Calakmul, a captive, possibly from Calakmul, is associated with the *Oxte'tun* sign (Stela 18, Morley 1937–38: pl. 153b), and a royal woman from Calakmul appears to have married into the local dynasty at some unspecified time in the Late

---

[6] Another context in which T606.23 **TAN-na** plays a role is that of the so-called half-period completion sign, which "denotes that half the next highest period (usually the katun, very rarely the baktun) is complete" (Thompson 1950: 192, figs. 32, 46–55). *Tan,* as *"el medio de una cosa"* (Barrera Vásquez 1980: 770), makes good sense in this context.

[7] There is at present no convincing evidence that the *"ik"* sign was in fact read **IK',** "wind." On iconographic grounds there are reasons for believing that the sign represents a floral or vegetal form.

[8] The reading order of the last two signs is confirmed by comparison with a common glyphic compound rendered as

either T671(586b) or T585b:671, yielding **pa-chi.** Evidently, Mayan spelling conventions dictated that the infixed element (T586b, in this instance) be read before the main sign.

[9] The attribution of monuments to the "snake-head" Emblem Glyph site carries with it some risk. For example, some of the monuments tabulated by Peter Mathews (n.d.c) in his compendium of such inscriptions are probably from subsidiary centers. This is made explicit on a number of panels, where relationship glyphs intervene between the names of the Site Q rulers and the local individuals who probably commissioned the panels.

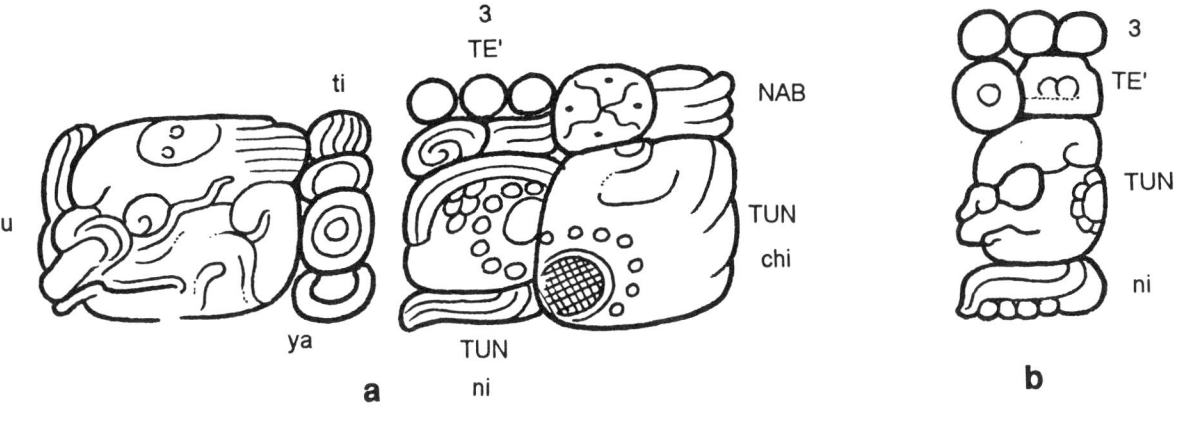

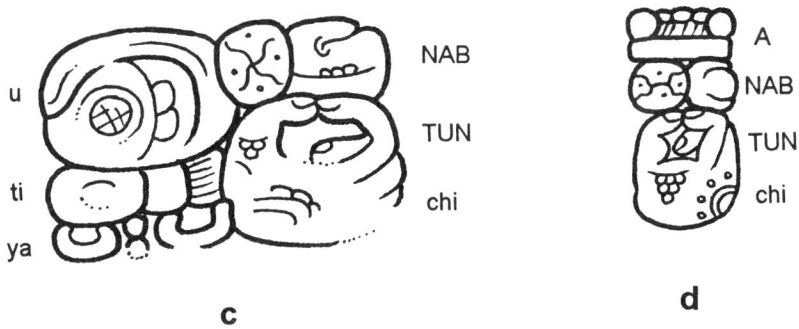

Fig. 29 Place names of Calakmul(?)

(a) unprovenanced panel, F3–F4 (after Schele and Miller 1986: pl. 101a)

(b) *Oxte'tun,* on Calakmul Stela 89:D5 (after drawing by Nikolai Grube, Mayer 1989: pl. 7)

(c) *Nabtunich,* on Dos Pilas Panel 7: B6 (drawing by Stephen D. Houston)

(d) *Nabtunich,* on Calakmul Stela 51: B3b (after unpublished drawing by Ian Graham).

Classic period (Stela 10, Morley 1937–38: pl. 151e). Unfortunately, the poor preservation of inscriptions at Calakmul makes it difficult to confirm the identification of the place names.

## Topoxte

A stela from Topoxte may show not only the Yaxha Emblem, which was apparently used around the Lake Yaxha, but the place name of Topoxte island and its environs (Fig. 31a). At the end of the text occurs an *ut-i* expression, in which the probable place glyph consists of the signs **CHAK,** a curious sign representing a shell, and the superfix **NAL,** complemented by a final **-la.** There is still some uncertainty as to whether these signs refer to Topoxte, because, as we have seen, the use of place names may also pinpoint the location of faraway events. The *"Chak-shell-nal"* place is also mentioned in two other texts: on a Late Classic vase published by Francis Robicsek (1978: pl. 145), and on Altar 5 at Tikal, in a poorly understood context (Fig. 31b).

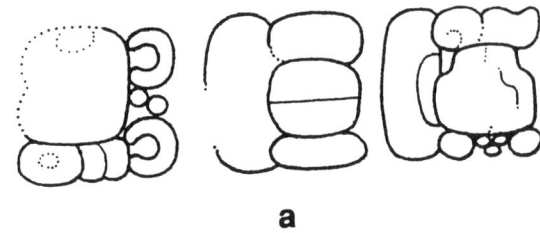

a

b

Fig. 30 Calakmul (?) place name on Naranjo Hieroglyphic Stairway 1: L3 (*CMHI* 2: 109).

Fig. 31 Topoxte place name

(a) Topoxte Stela 1 (drawn after original)
(b) place name on Tikal Altar 5 (after Jones and Satterthwaite 1982: fig. 23).

## Palenque

Another place glyph apparently refers to Palenque (Fig. 32). It consists of two signs, T262 representing some type of foliage, and the **HA** element already familiar to us from the Dos Pilas place glyph. Throughout the inscriptions of Palenque, particularly in the texts of the Cross Group, this glyph consistently occurs after *ut-i* in appended sentences.

Based on a new decipherment of the "foliage" sign by one of the authors (Stuart), we believe we can offer a full phonetic transliteration of the toponym as **LAKAM-HA.** The **LAKAM** value of the foliage is suggested by several lines of evidence that would take too much space to describe here; suffice it to say that the sign also appears in another place glyph read **LAKAM-TUN,** associated with an unknown site near the Pasion and Usumacinta Rivers (Fig. 41). It seems reasonable to suppose that this glyph corresponds to the familiar and old geographical name Lacantun, "Big Stone" (the origin of the term "Lacandon"), as

the Lacantun River joins the Usumacinta near its confluence with the Pasion. (More on this particular Lacantun place glyph is discussed under the section "Titles of Origin.")

Returning to the Palenque glyph under discussion, we can similarly see that the place glyph **LAKAM-HA** recalls the modern toponym Lacanha ("Big Water"), which is the name of a site and a nearby river some distance to the south, near the Lacantun River. Given the distance between modern Palenque and Lacanha, we would not venture to suggest that the place glyph at Palenque is historically related to Lacanha. We would suggest, however, that the designation "Big Water" may have been general enough to have referred to many places in the ancient Maya landscape. The same **LAKAM-HA** glyph appears on Lintel 4 of Bonampak (Fig. 33), a war memorial, where it refers to some individual as **A-LAKAM-HA,** or *Ah Lakamha', "He of Lakamha'."* This reference can be interpreted in one of two ways: either the

LAKAM HA'

Fig. 32 Palenque place name, Tablet of the Foliated Cross: M14b (drawing by Linda Schele in Lounsbury 1980: fig. 2).

individual mentioned is from Palenque, and therefore indicates an early war between Bonampak and Palenque, or, more interestingly, perhaps, the title actually refers to a defeated noble from the site we today call Lacanha (or sometimes Kuna-Lacanha), named for the lake and river located just to the west of Bonampak. The second interpretation would rest on the assumption that the modern toponym Lacanha is a very old one, and indeed it was at least in use in colonial times (de Vos 1980: 509). However we choose to interpret the Bonampak reference, we feel fairly confident in assigning the name *Lakamha'* to ancient Palenque. "Big Water" may have referred to the extensive waterfalls and pools of the Otulum River that are today visible at the site, and which no doubt attracted its original inhabitants.

In Figure 34 we find an elaboration on the *Lakamha'* place name, with the addition of several glyphs between *ut-i* and the toponym. These intervening signs are **ye-ma-la K'UK'-LAKAM wi-tsi,** which probably spell *Yemalk'uk' Lakamwits,* or "Descending Quetzal Big Hill." The *Lakamha'* name follows directly afterwards, then the "sky-bone." Here we may have an extended version of the Palenque toponym, but it is equally likely that the additional elements specify a place within the site proper. This and other glyphs for site areas will be discussed more fully in Chapter 6.

Another less common place glyph occurs in the Palenque inscriptions. This can be phonetically transcribed **to-ko-TAN-na,** or *Toktan.* The Tablet of the Sun records this as the location where Kan Xul I, an Early Classic ruler of Palenque, became heir (Fig. 35a; Schele 1984b). On the Palace Tablet, *Toktan* appears in *Toktan winik,* "*Toktan* man," apparently an epithet for Kan Xul II (Fig. 35b). Like the *ahaw* title and the prefix *ah, winik* seems to be a titular term that can be modified through the addition of a place name.

## Piedras Negras

Another place name may designate Piedras Negras (Fig. 36). Preceded by the *ut-i* expression and followed by the "sky compound," it appears in only two secure contexts, both from the inscription of the eroded Altar 1. The place glyph is very similar to the variable elements in the Piedras Negras Emblem Glyph (**yo-ki-bi**), suggesting that this is another instance of overlap between Emblem Glyphs and place names. *Yokib* may well signify "entrance" (cf. Slocum and Gerdel 1976: 168; and the Tzeltal place name *Yochib,* Berlin, Breedlove, and Raven 1974: 21), possibly in reference to the location of the site astride the entrance of a valley, or to a sinkhole in the vicinity.

Other place names occur on Hieroglyphic Throne 1 of Piedras Negras (Figs. 36c–g; Thompson 1950: fig. 58). Two include the *na,* "house," glyph (alternately spelled **na** and **na-h(V),** Figs. 36c–e), and one is followed by the **yo-OTOT,** "his house," sign (Fig. 36e)—presumably, then, these were the names of structures (see Chap. 6). The other place names (Figs. 36f–g) occur after verbs (Chap. 3, including the glyph "to arrive"); one accompanies the **TAN-**"bone" sign (Fig.

A LAKAM HA'

Fig. 33 Bonampak Lintel 4: A1–E4 (after unpublished drawing by Ian Graham).

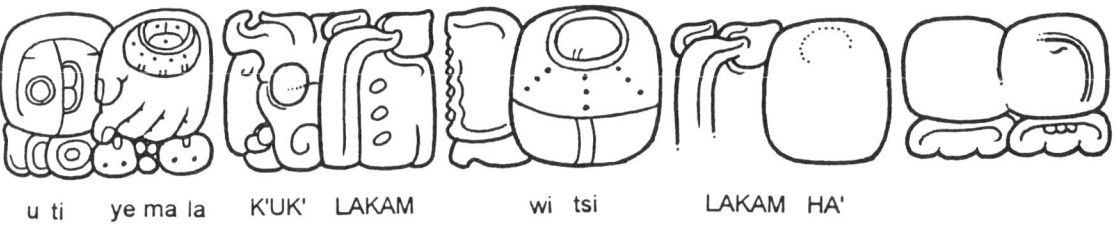

u ti   ye ma la   K'UK' LAKAM   wi tsi   LAKAM HA'

Fig. 34 Extended place name at Palenque, Temple 18, Doorjamb: D17–D19 (drawing by David Stuart from photographs).

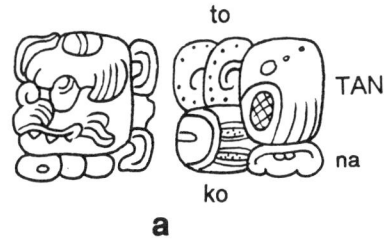

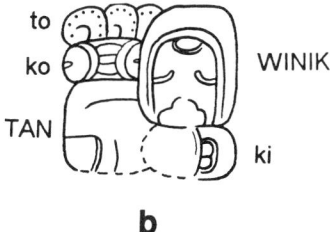

a                              b

Fig. 35 *Toktan* at Palenque

(a) Tablet of the Sun: Q4–P5 (drawing by Linda Schele in Lounsbury 1980: fig. 3)

(b) Palace Tablet: D17 (drawing by Linda Schele in Robertson 1985: pl. 258).

36g), suggesting that it, too, is a toponym. Most of these place names may refer to wings, rooms, or substructures of the palace where the throne was found. And one (Fig. 36g) may well pertain to the nearby site of El Cayo, inasmuch as the toponym makes an appearance on El Cayo Panel 1 (Maler 1903: pl. xxxv).

## Machaquila

A final place glyph to be discussed here is composed of T510bv(501): 23, which evidently refers to the site of Machaquila. The sign consists of a quatrefoil-shaped glyph that surrounds a darkened *imix,* or **HA** ("water") glyph. In some examples the two elements are separated, showing that *ha'* is the final element. Although this glyph is very common at Machaquila, other sites may have used a similar place name. On Seibal Stela 8, for example, the glyph appears after the *ut-i* verb (Fig. 37b). Nonetheless, three monuments at Machaquila (Stelae 4, 7, and 8), all roughly contemporary with the Seibal stela, depict the glyph below the feet of local rulers (two are shown in Figs. 37a,c).[10] The parallel with toponyms in basal registers at Aguateca and Dos Pilas is striking enough to warrant its identification as a place name.

On a parenthetical note, the center of the main plaza of Machaquila shows an unusual feature described by Ian Graham: ". . . a quatrefoil-shaped area, depressed some 0.2 m below the level of its surroundings, is edged with well finished stones" (Fig. 38; Graham 1967: 59). The similarity to the Machaquila toponym is unlikely to be coincidental. Might this have been a large version of the place glyph, decorating the floor of the plaza?

To summarize, place names for several Maya sites have been proposed based on their association with the *ut-i* expression. However, these are not the only places noted by the Maya in their inscriptions. With the material presented so far, we may now analyze in detail another aspect of Maya toponymy: titles of origin.

## Titles of Origin

When accompanying a personal name, the place glyphs associated with Dos Pilas, Naranjo, and other sites may take the prefix sign **A** (either T12 or T229), which surely represents the male agentive prefix *ah-,* "he of . . . ." This morpheme works in Mayan languages to signify, among

---

[10] Stela 7, shown in Fig. 27c, is doubly interesting, for it refers not only to the placement of the monument (D1), but to the fact that, 35 days later, someone—presumably the ruler—**IL-ba,** "saw himself." We suspect that this event refers to an unveiling ceremony and possibly to the amount of time required to carve a monument with the ruler's portrait after the erection of a blank stela.

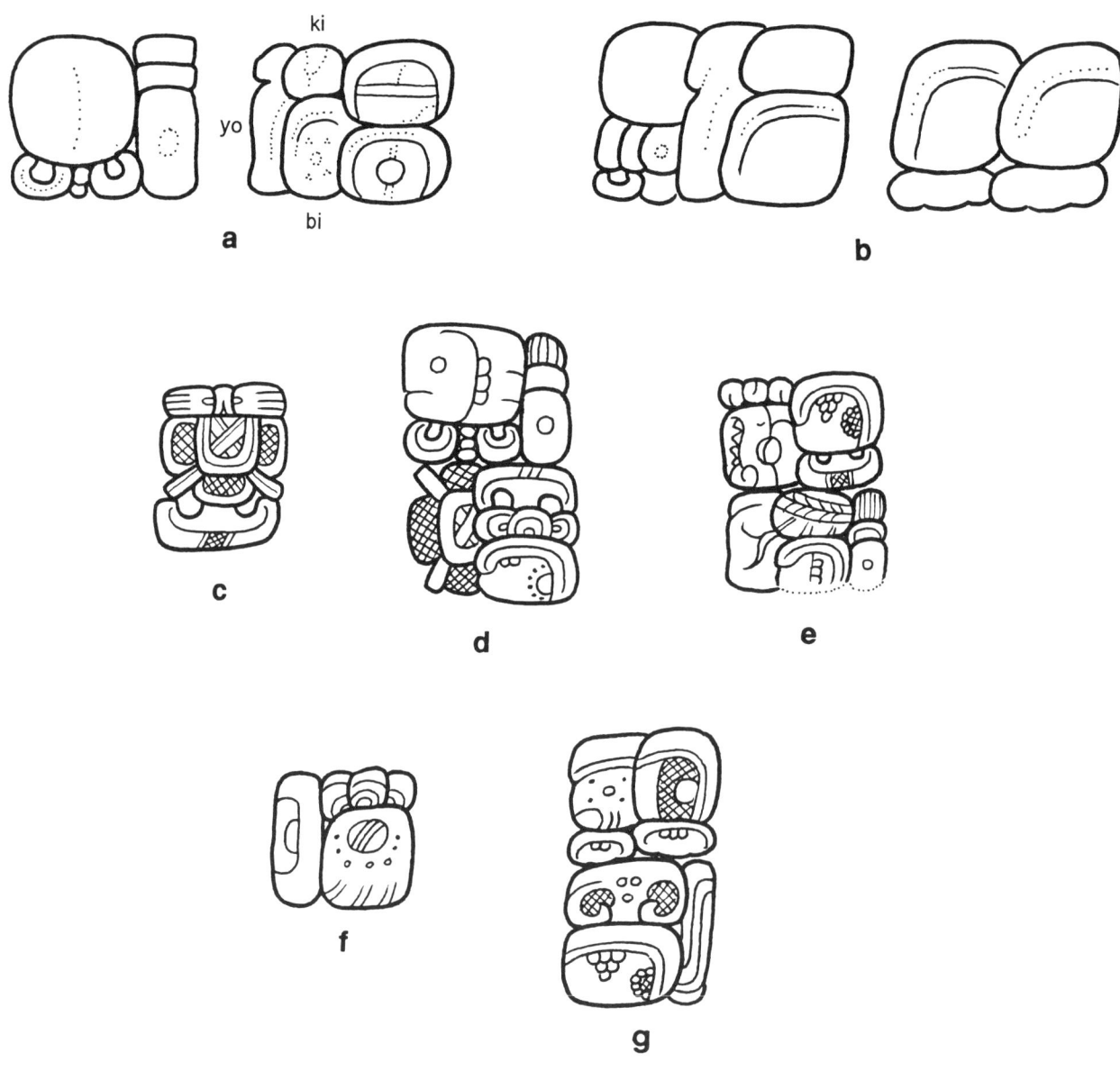

Fig. 36 Piedras Negras place names

(a) Altar 1: H2–I2 (after Morley 1937–38: pl. 144)
(b) Altar 1: Y2–Z2 (after Morley 1937–38: pl. 144)
(c) Throne 1: D'1 (after Thompson 1950: fig. 58)
(d) Throne 1: E'2–E'3 (after Thompson 1950: fig. 58)

(e) Throne 1: K'4–K'5 (after Thompson 1950: fig. 58)
(f) Throne 1: F'5 (after Thompson 1950: fig. 58)
(g) Throne 1: F'1–F'2 (after Thompson 1950: fig. 58).

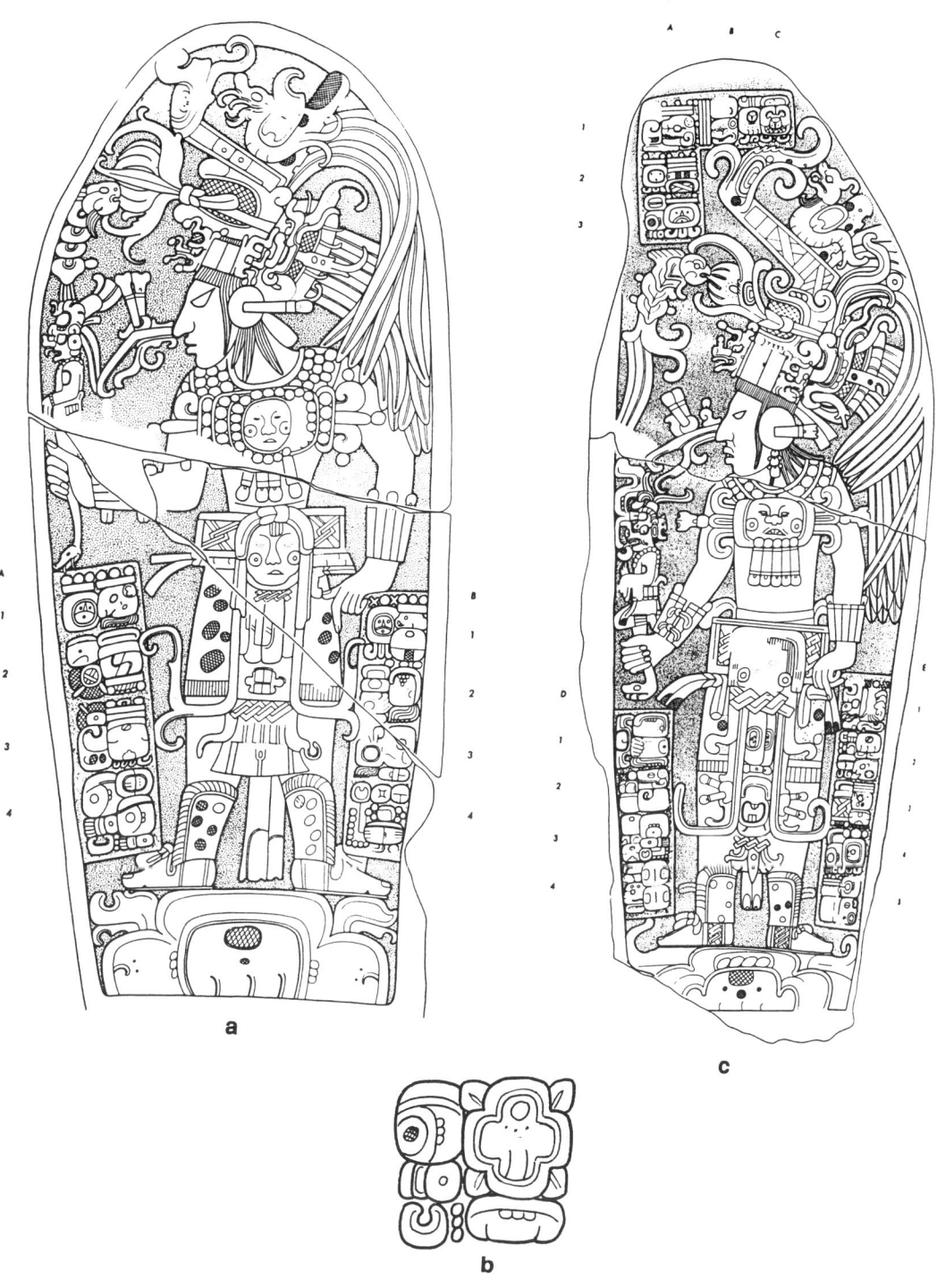

a

b

c

Fig. 37 Machaquila place name

(a) Machaquila Stela 4 (I. Graham 1967: fig. 51)
(b) Seibal Stela 8: C5 (after Maler 1908b: pl. 7)

(c) Machaquila Stela 7 (I. Graham 1967: fig. 57).

35

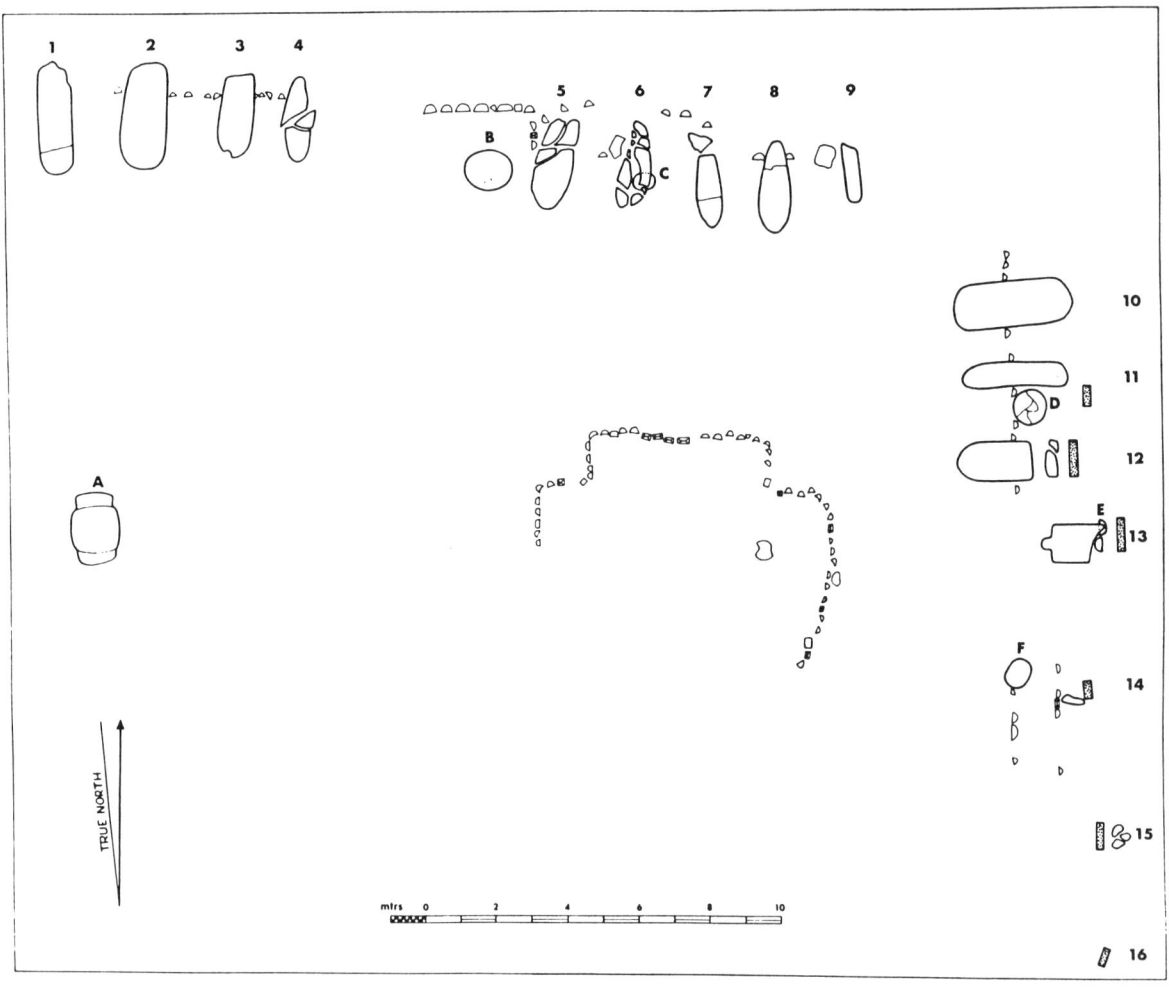

Fig. 38 Plan of Machaquila Plaza (I. Graham 1967: fig. 42).

other things, the place of origin of an individual. *Ah Kumk'al,* for example, refers to a native of Kumk'al (Conkal) (Barrera Vásquez 1980: 3). The hieroglyphic pattern of **A-**[place glyph] therefore perfectly fits the established usage, and such glyphs can be grouped under the category of "titles of origin." While we have already touched on this category with a few specific examples, the time has come for a more lengthy treatment of this pattern. As we hope to demonstrate, a fair number of glyphs with the **A-** prefix appear to "behave" like place glyphs—even as an Emblem Glyph in one case—even though we never find

them in association with the *ut-i* verb, our only criterion for identifying place glyphs thus far.

A useful illustration of such "suggestive" place glyphs comes from Lintel 16 from Yaxchilan, where a captive takes the title **A-wa-k'a-bi,** possibly for *Ah Wak'ab* (Fig. 39, A3). He is then named as a subordinate lord of one *Lakam Chaak,* a "Lord of *Wak'ab* (**wa-k'a-bi-AHAW**) (Fig. 39, E1). The latter title is in essence a simple Emblem Glyph, leading us to suspect that *Wak'ab* refers to some location in the general vicinity of the Usumacinta River.

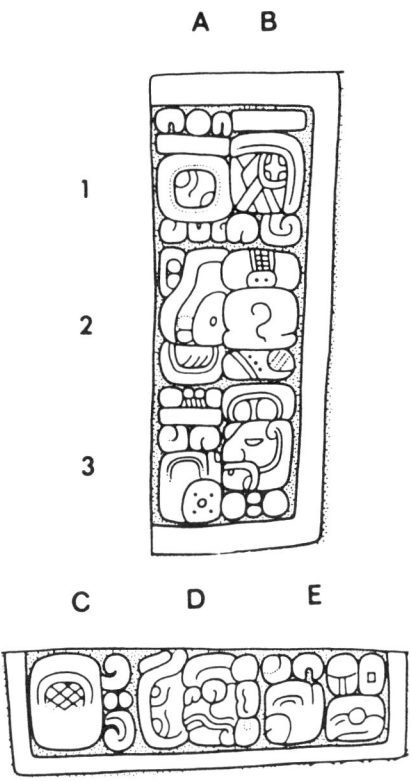

A     B

1

2

3

C     D     E

Fig. 39 *Wak'ab* place name on Yaxchilan Lintel 16, note especially A3 and E1 (*CMHI* 3: 41).

Monuments from the site of El Chorro, located north of the Pasion River, exhibit another title which is probably based on a place glyph (Fig. 40) (Houston 1986: 3–5). The unusual compound appears to consist of the superfix for the "Pictun" period (of unknown value), followed by **ni(-la).** In most instances we find this modified with -*ahaw* (Fig. 40b), but a few carry the *ah*- agentive prefix, and are thus probably read "He of El Chorro."

In the same area of the Usumacinta and Pasion Rivers we find an Emblem Glyph and title of origin composed of the signs **LAKAM** and **TUN**

(see the earlier discussion of Palenque's place name) (Fig. 41a–e). In the texts of Itzan, Guatemala, the name *Lakamtun* occurs with both *ah*- (Fig. 41b) and -*ahaw* (Fig. 41d), presumably depending on the rank of the person using the epithet; those of higher rank would have been "lords" of the location, and others would simply have originated there. The precise location of *Lakamtun* is unknown, but references to it at Yaxchilan, Itzan, and Seibal suggest that it lies somewhere in the Usumacinta–Pasion region. It is tempting to relate this hieroglyphic name to the modern term Lacantun, which refers to a major river flowing into the Usumacinta and, in Colonial times, to a lake in lowland Chiapas that today goes by the name Lago Miramar. Lacantun, "Big Rock," is an old name, but whether it can be extended back into the Classic period remains to be proved.

At Seibal we find an example of *Lakamtun* as an Emblem Glyph (Fig. 41a), which to our knowledge has previously gone unrecognized. The "title of origin" form may appear at Itzan (Fig. 41d) with the addition of the agentive *ah*- prefix (*Ah Lakamtun*, "He of *Lakamtun*"). With the -*ahaw* title it appears to name a captive at Yaxchilan portrayed within a ball, bound and trussed into an arched, uncomfortable posture (Fig. 41e).

Slightly further downstream, at the site of Piedras Negras, are references to a place we call "Rabbit Stone" (perhaps *T'ultun*), so read because of the two components of their glyphs. An important retainer of the last-known lord at the site was the *ahaw* of this place (Fig. 42a), and another individual mentioned on Piedras Negras Stela 40 merely came from "Rabbit Stone," at least to judge from the "*Ah*-Rabbit Stone" expression on the side of the monument (Fig. 42b). The location of this place cannot be pinpointed, although it must surely have been in the neighborhood of Piedras Negras.

A point worth mentioning about titles of origin is that they occasionally accompany Emblem Glyphs. In one example, from the neighborhood of Tamarindito and Arroyo de Piedra, a ruler was both the *Ch'ul ahaw* or "Holy Lord" of the local polity and **A-CHAK-HA,** or *Ah Chakha'*, "He of

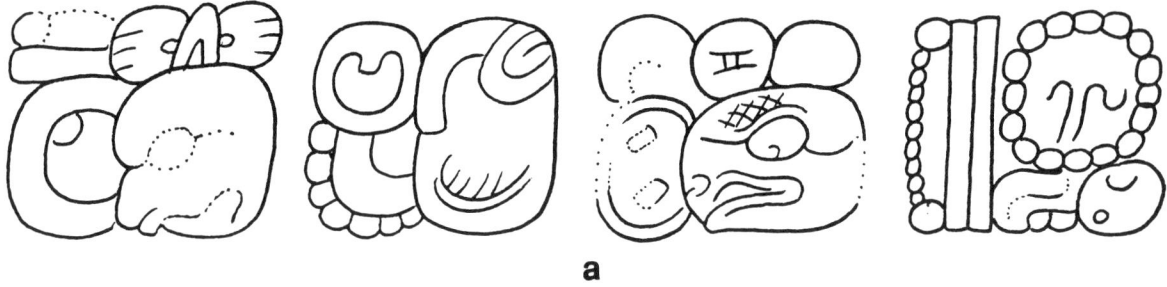

a

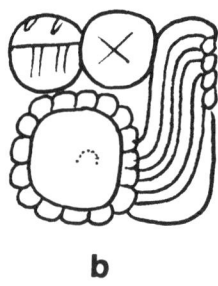

b

Fig. 40 Title of origin at El Chorro

(a) stela from El Chorro area, A6–B3 (after
    unpublished drawing by Ian Graham)

(b) unprovenanced stela from El Chorro area, A9
    (after unpublished drawing by Ian Graham).

the Red (or Great) Water" (Fig. 43a). A woman who married into the same dynasty employed the title *Chakha' Ahaw;* that is, she was a high-ranking person from "Red Water" (Fig. 43c). We suspect, first, that *Chakha'* refers to what is known today as the Riachuelo Chacrio, a stream running within 3 km of Arroyo de Piedra. (The name is apt: during the rainy season the stream becomes deep red from the suspended sediment being washed downstream.) Second, *Chakha'* may have been the seat of a small polity north of Tamarindito and Arroyo de Piedra; possibly, the ruler was even born there. Unfortunately, we cannot yet determine the status of *Chakha'* relative to Arroyo de Piedra and Tamarindito. Our hunch is that *Chakha'* began as the center of an independent polity and was incorporated later into the larger polity to the south.

A similar pattern of place names and Emblem Glyphs occurs in the area of Bonampak and Lacanha. On the Lacanha panel in the Dumbarton Oaks collection (Fig. 44a), an overlord uses the two Emblems of the local polity (D4). Yet he is also characterized as "He of the 'Knot' " (D5), the "knot" being an unidentified glyph that Houston once linked to the main sign of the Dos Pilas Emblem (Houston and Mathews 1985: fig. 9). As Joel Palka (personal communication, 1990) points out to us, Houston was mistaken. Rather, the "knot" represents a probable toponym, found also as part of a woman's name—a lady *ahaw* of the "knot" site—at El Chorro, where she appears to have been the mother of a local ruler (Fig. 44b). The "knot site" may lie somewhere between El Chorro and Lacanha, near the upper reaches of the Usumacinta River.

The position of titles of origin after Emblem Glyphs is fairly consistent, although there is one example that probably came before (Fig. 45). The title **A-SAK-NIK-TE,** or *Ah Saknikte'* "He of White Flower," precedes the local Emblem (see later discussion). Although it remains to be proved, "White Flower" may be a place within a particular polity.

Before leaving titles of origin, especially as they relate to Emblems, it is important to stress that they may also follow the titles of members of the nobility. The only clear illustration of this pattern comes from El Cayo (Fig. 46). Panel 1 shows that one place—the evident burial location of a lord of El Cayo (Fig. 46a, see discussion in Chap. 3)—is also mentioned in a title of origin following a subsidiary title (Fig. 46b; D. Stuart n.d.a).

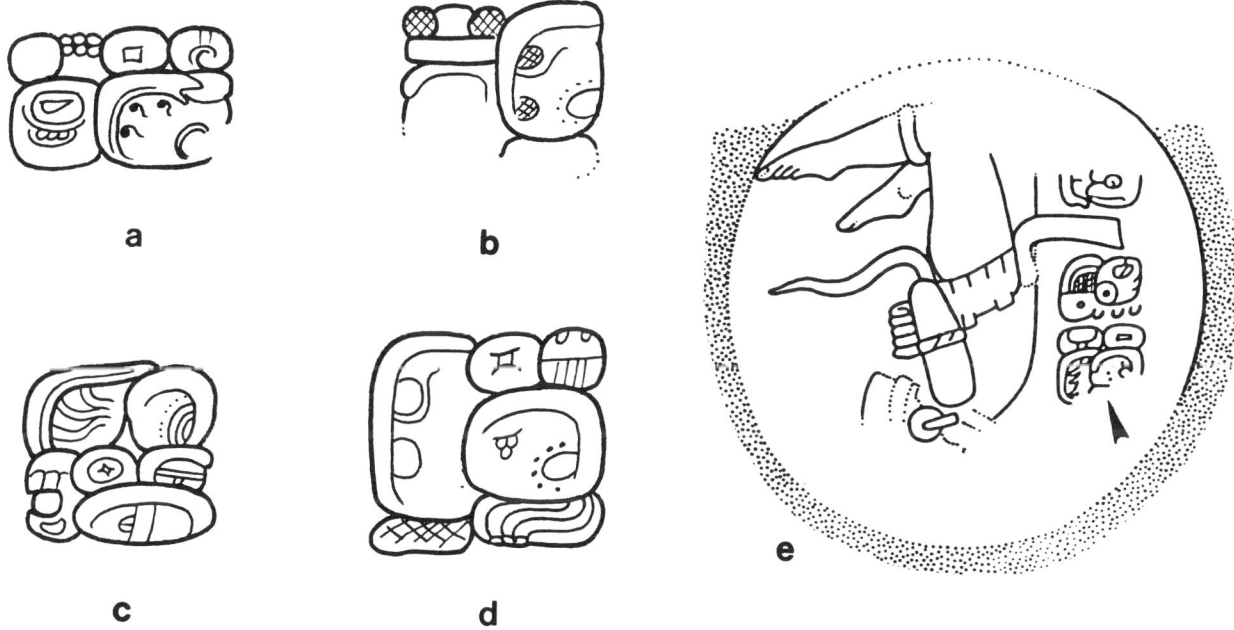

Fig. 41  The "*Lakamtun*" place name

(a) Emblem Glyph or Seibal Stela 9: D4 (drawing from photograph by David Stuart)
(b) "He of *Lakamtun*," Itzan Stela 17: L6 (after unpublished drawing by Ian Graham)
(c) "*ahaw* of *Lakamtun*," Yaxchilan Lintel 35 (*CMHI* 3: 79)

(d) "*ahaw* of *Lakamtun*," on Itzan Stela 17: K3 (after unpublished drawing by Ian Graham)
(e) captive termed an *ahaw* of "*Lakamtun*," Yaxchilan Hieroglyphic Stairway 2: S1–4 (*CMHI* 3: 16).

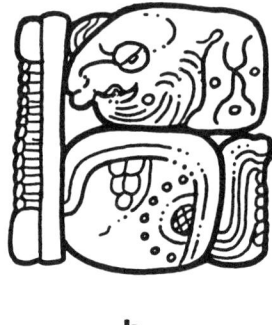

**a**          **b**

Fig. 42 The "Rabbit Stone" place name

(a) *ahaw* of the "Rabbit Stone," on Piedras Negras Throne 1: O'1 (drawn after original in the Museo Nacional de Arqueología e Etnología)

(b) "He of the Rabbit Stone," on Piedras Negras Stela 40: C11 (after Thompson 1950: fig. 58).

**a**

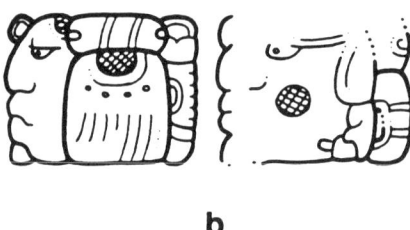

**b**          **c**

Fig. 43 The *Chakha'* place name, in titles of origin

(a) Arroyo de Piedra Stela 2: G2–G4 (after unpublished drawing by Stephen Houston)

(b) Altar de Sacrificios Sculptured Panel 1: A4 (after J. Graham 1972: fig. 57)

(c) Tamarindito Hieroglyphic Stairway 3: Step 5, e (after unpublished drawing by Stephen Houston).

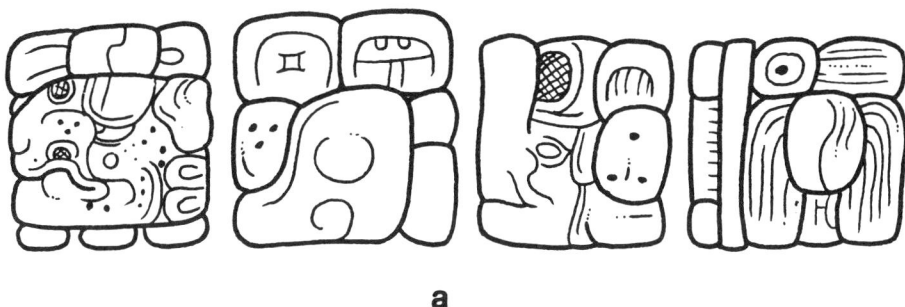

a

b

Fig. 44 People from the "knot" site

(a) Lacanha Panel 1: C4–D5 (drawing by David Stuart)

(b) Lady of the "knot site," El Chorro Altar 6 (after unpublished drawing by Eric von Euw).

SAK

A

NIK       TE'

Fig. 45 "He of *Saknikte'* " (after Kerr 1990: 276).

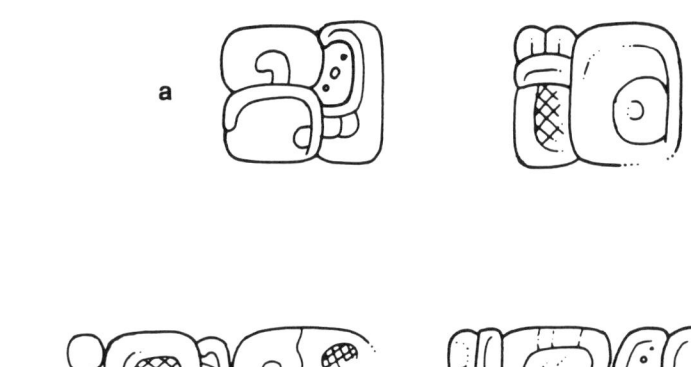

Fig. 46 Hieroglyphs from El Cayo Panel 1
(a) burial verb, D12–C14

(b) title of origin with local lord, M11–N13 (both
figures after Maler 1903: pl. 35).

CHAPTER 3

# Place Names with Other Verbs

Sometimes the location of a particular event is included in the sentence proper and not in a separate phrase introduced by *ut-i*. Perhaps the clearest example of this is the so-called shell-star verb that somehow refers to intersite war; the location of a battle or skirmish is either mentioned directly afterward or conflated with the verb itself (Fig. 47). This custom of naming the location of an event after a verb reflects the pattern where *ut-i* precedes place glyphs, but in a more compact fashion—in a sense, *ut-i,* "it happened (at . . .)," is simply a restatement of a verb mentioned in the primary clause.

Such phrasing has long been documented elsewhere in Maya script. In the Venus pages of the Dresden Codex, the set glyphic phrase for the appearance of Venus as morning star consists of a verb ("mirror-over-hand," the meaning of which is not known), followed by one of the four cardinal directions (Fig. 48). The name of the subject follows, along with the name *Chak Ek'*. In other examples the direction glyph appears after the name of the subject, demonstrating that directional glyphs, the functional equivalent of place names, may "float" within a sentence, yet without leading to substantial changes in meaning. We should stress that locatives, which ordinarily might be expected in this context, do not accompany the directional glyphs in the Dresden Codex.

Perhaps, as with place glyphs, locative prepositions were optional in certain phrases, or possibly they were spoken but not written.

Similar patterns exist in monumental inscriptions. At Dos Pilas, for example, the local place glyph often follows verbs besides *ut-i*. The "shell-star" reference on Hieroglyphic Stairway 2 is one good example (see previous discussion, Fig. 47b), another being the record of Ruler 2's burial on the back of Stela 8 (H13–I15; Fig. 49a). The verb at H14 is clear—*muk-ah,* "was buried" (Mathews n.d.c)—and the name of the subject comes two glyphs later, in the form of "3 Katun *ahaw,* Ruler 2," at H15b and I15. Between these parts of the sentence is a reference to the location of the burial itself, expressed with the same glyphs found in an earlier *ut-i* phrase on Stela 8 (H21–H22); a similar pattern occurs on El Cayo Panel 1, which contains a burial verb (Mathews n.d.c) and both general and specific place references (Fig. 46). Conceivably, the burial of Ruler 2 took place in the central area of Dos Pilas and not at one of the many outlying sites within the local polity. Excavations by the Vanderbilt Petexbatun Project into a likely burial spot, Structure L5-1, have found a royal tomb that, on the evidence of physical anthropology, matches closely the expected age at death of Ruler 2. Regrettably, glyphic material from the tomb fails to confirm the identification.

**a**

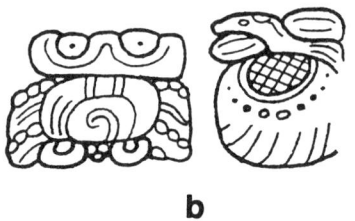
**b**

Fig. 47 Shell-star events

(a) "shell-star" at Yaxha, from Tikal Temple 4 (Structure 5C–4), Lintel 3: B4 (Jones and Satterthwaite 1982: fig. 74)

(b) "shell-star" at Dos Pilas, from Dos Pilas Hieroglyphic Stairway 2: A2b–B1a, east (after unpublished drawing by Ian Graham).

A glyph at Piedras Negras may specify the location of another royal burial (Fig. 49b). On Lintel 3 at Piedras Negras, Peter Mathews (n.d.c) identified a passage that recorded not only the death of a local ruler (Ruler 4), but his burial three days later. Immediately after the "was buried" verb—and in conformity with the example from Dos Pilas—is a glyph that includes a "shield" element and a **WITS**, "hill," logograph; the name of the ruler follows. The reference to a hill is unlikely to allude to the person connected to this event but is rather part of a word order consisting of verb-location-subject.

An identical pattern is present in a burial reference painted in Tomb 12 at Rio Azul (Fig. 49c). After the glyph "was buried" is a phrase we shall refer to as *wak kaan muyal nal,* or "Six Sky Clouds," followed by the name of the tomb's occupant.

The **MUYAL** reading deserves further discussion. Page 68a of the Dresden Codex shows two Chaaks, one bathed by streams of water, the other not (Fig. 50). The space above them shares a dotted curlicue, T632. In our view, this sign represents the sign for *muyal,* "cloud," so that the Chaaks are sitting beneath cloudy skies, one already drenched with rain. In at least three places, phonetic clues point to this reading; several spellings end in the syllables **ya-la,** and one begins

with **mu** (Figs. 51a–c). In short, both T632 and its iconographic versions at Ixlu, Copan, and elsewhere represent clouds, as seems appropriate given their position above the heads of rulers and deities.[11]

In view of the parallels from Dos Pilas and Piedras Negras, we believe that *wak kaan muyal nal* refers to the location of Tomb 12, perhaps an area or building within Rio Azul (*pace* Stuart 1987a); interestingly, the same place name is also attested in a contemporary text on El Zapote Stela 5: C9–D9, although this time with an apparent **WITS** glyph (Fig. 52). Other tombs at Rio Azul are inscribed with hill names, each standing alone on one of three walls. Unfortunately, the tombs have not yet been fully published, so their discussion must await a future occasion.

Aside from the *ut-i,* shell-star, and burial expressions, there are other glyphic phrases that include place names. The first of these occurs at Palenque and Tikal; it consists of T79 over the syllables **la** and **ha** and probably serves as a verb (Figs. 53a–b). In some inscriptions at Palenque this glyph introduces a short clause at the end of an inscription, a pattern that brings the *ut-i* expression to mind. There are two other similarities as well: *Lakamha',* the presumed place name of Palenque, usually follows the glyph to close the inscription; and the "sky-bone" compound, an integral part

---

[11] The cloud interpretation of the dotted S-shape motifs on the Terminal Classic monuments from Ixlu, Jimbal, and

Ucanal revises their previous identification as blood scrolls by one of the authors (Stuart 1984).

Fig. 48 Dresden Codex Venus page 46 (Villacorta and Villacorta 1930: 102).

of many place-name references, sometimes makes an appearance (Fig. 53a). Most likely, then, the verb functions in the same way as the *ut-i* clause, although, to be sure, its precise meaning may be different.

Another occurrence of the T79 **-la-ha** verb is at Tikal (Fig. 53b), where the expression helps identify a local place name. The presumed place name contains the main sign of the Tikal Emblem Glyph, a **YAX** superfix, and other, less familiar components. We suspect that the main sign of the Tikal Emblem served originally as the place name of the site. Only later did it grow to become a polity label.

Another verbal glyph functions quite like **u-ti-ya** by introducing brief locational sentences that follow longer passages. In all respects such phrases work like the place name formula described in the first chapter and illustrated in Figure 6. The only minor difference is in the verbal glyph itself, where the **u** sign is replaced by a skeletal sign with a "chuen" infix (Fig. 54). The **-ti-ya** signs follow in precisely the same manner as in **u-ti-ya.** We feel there is a strong possibility that the "chuen-skull" is a logograph read **UH,** for **UH-ti-ya,** a variant spelling of *ut-i*. The insertion of the /**h**/ probably reflects the proto-Cholan form *\*uht-i* (Schumann 1973: 98; Kaufmann and Norman 1984: 135).

Fig. 49 Burial references

(a) Dos Pilas Stela 8: H13–I15 (after unpublished drawing by Ian Graham)

(b) Piedras Negras, Lintel 3: V6–V7 (after Thompson 1950: fig. 57)

(c) Rio Azul Tomb 12 (after Stuart 1987a: fig. 45).

Fig. 50 Dresden Codex page 68a, showing Chaaks in clouds (Villacorta and Villacorta 1930: 146).

The evidence in support of the reading is as follows. Many ornaments, including several ex-amples of jade from Chichen Itza, display "name-tags"—glyphs recording the name of a possessed object, ranging from houses to bones (Mathews 1979; Houston, Stuart, and Taube 1989; Houston 1989). At Chichen the texts begin with **yu-UH-il,** for *y-uh-il,* the possessed form of *uh,* "neck-lace" (Sapper 1907: 445; Josserand and Hopkins n.d.: 9), doubtless because all objects described as *uh* are drilled for suspension, probably as neck ornaments (Fig. 55a, an unprovenanced example in Fig. 55b). We propose that the "chuen-skull" was used as a logograph in such spellings; it also served to record the aspirate in the proto-Cholan root *uht.*[12]

A clear example of how this compound works is in the texts of Pomona, Tabasco, Mexico. In at least two places *uht-i* is followed by an apparent place name, **pi-a** (Figs. 56a–b). Much like several toponyms discussed previously, this name may also serve as the main sign of an Emblem Glyph (Fig. 56c).

The spelling of the sign deserves further com-ment, for it touches on an important feature of Maya spelling: the use of two small dots—a min-iature "two"—to indicate that a phonetic sign or, more seldom, a logograph should be read twice. This relatively rare feature of the script involves the attachment of two small dots to the sign in question, usually on its upper left corner, more rarely on its upper right; in transliterations we designate the doubled feature with a superscript 2.[13] Figure 57 shows many such spellings: (1) **ka²-wa** for **ka-ka-wa,** *kakaw* or "chocolate" (Figs. 57a–b); (2) **k'u²** for **k'u-k'u,** *k'uk'* or "quetzal" (Fig. 57c); (3) **u-ne²** for **u-ne-ne,** *unen* or "child," a label for GII of the Palenque Triad (Fig. 57d).

[12] *Uh* for "collar ornament" is also spelled on the central panel, for example, in position B8 of the Temple of the In-scriptions at Palenque (Fig. 55c). The spelling at Palenque differs from the examples at Chichen Itza, in that here it reads **u-h(V),** an unpossessed form, occasionally inflected as a ver-bal noun. What is intriguing at Palenque is that the glyph for "collar ornament" is commonly paired with **tu-pa,** *tup,*

"earspool, ear ornament" (Mathews 1979). D. Stuart has long felt that this text refers to the dressing of deity effigies with jewelry and other regalia.

[13] We do not yet understand why some spellings use this convention. Perhaps they signal a particular spelling when two are possible: **chi-K'IN** in place of **K'IN-chi,** or **k'a-k'a** instead of **BUTS',** respectively.

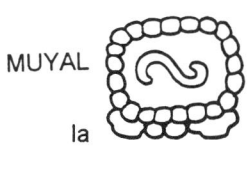

**a**  **b**  **c**

Fig. 51 Evidence for the *muyal* reading

(a) Piedras Negras Lintel 2: G'1 (drawing by David Stuart)

(b) glyph on unprovenanced vessel referring to Naranjo ruler (after Kerr 1990: 214)

(c) glyph from unprovenanced vessel (M. Coe 1973: 113).

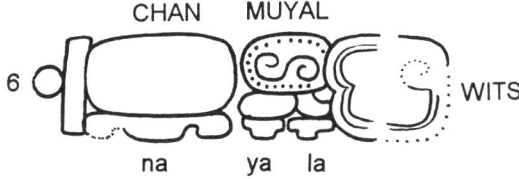

Fig. 52 Hieroglyphs from El Zapote Stela 5: C9–D9 (after unpublished drawing by Ian Graham).

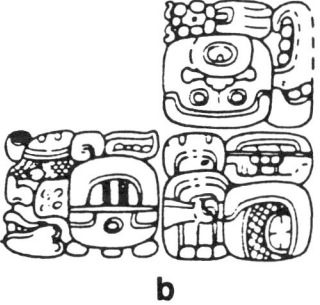

**a**  **b**

Fig. 53 Dedication verb

(a) Palenque Temple of the Foliated Cross, Alfarda, K1–L2 (drawing by Linda Schele in Lounsbury 1980: fig. 5)

(b) Tikal Temple 4 (Structure 5C–4), Lintel 3, H3–H4 (Jones and Satterthwaite 1982: fig. 74).

47

Fig. 54 The "chuen-skull" event, from Tikal Stela 31:
C6 (Jones and Satterthwaite 1982: fig. 52).

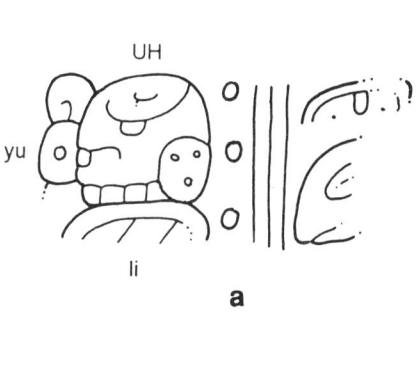

a

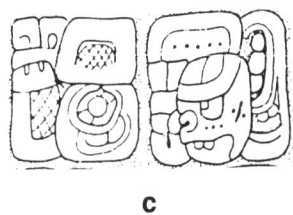

c

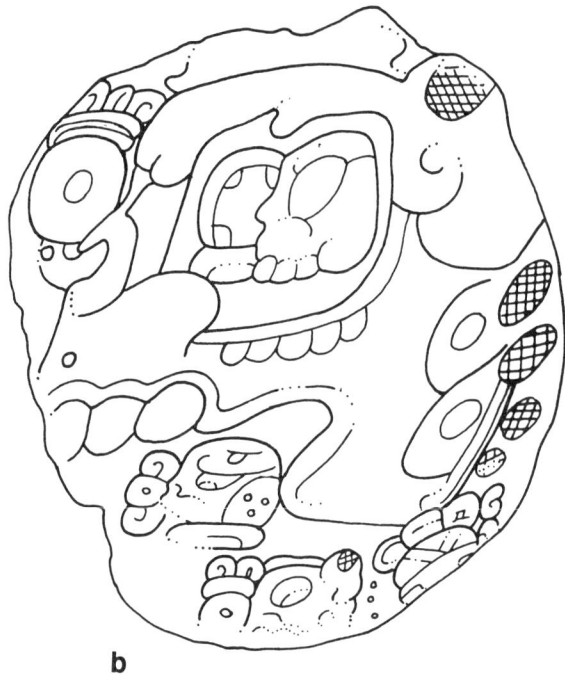

b

Fig. 55 A name tag for "pendants"

(a) Chichen Itza (after Proskouriakoff 1974: fig. 12)
(b) from unprovenanced item of shell jewelry (after
    Schele and Miller 1986: pl. 85)

(c) Palenque Temple of the Inscriptions, Middle Panel:
    B8–A9 (Robertson 1983: fig. 96).

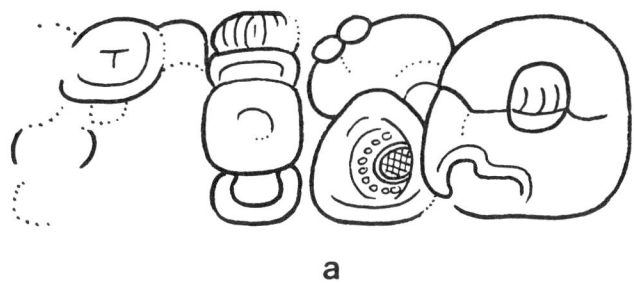

a

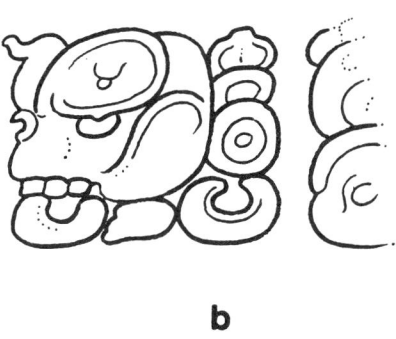

b

c

Fig. 56 Place name from Pomona

(a) Pomona panel (after unpublished drawing by Ian Graham)

(b) Pomona panel (after unpublished drawing by Ian Graham)

(c) Pomona Panel "X" (after Lizardi Ramos 1963: fig. 6).

**Pi²-A,** then, is simply another such spelling. Probably the final element was to be understood as *ha',* "a body of water," in reference to some natural feature near Pomona, possibly a section of the Usumacinta River.[14]

The inscription where the "chuen-skull" compound is most frequent is Stela 31 at Tikal. Figure 58 illustrates all such expressions from the text, along with their associated dates. In our opinion, the glyphs that immediately follow the "chuen-skull" are possible place names, although the places to which they refer remain in question. Of special interest are the glyphs at Figure 58a, which Peter Mathews has identified as a personal name (Mathews 1985: 44). The same glyphs appear directly after the accession verb on the famous Leiden plaque (Schele and Miller 1986: pl. 33), where they appear to serve, *pace* Mathews, as the place name of an area or building within Tikal. A more probable candidate for the personal name on Stela 31 is "Jester God-Jaguar," whose name glyphs appear in an iconographic context on Tikal Stela 29, possibly in association with an ancestral figure (Jones and Satterthwaite 1982: fig. 49).

[14] This place is also mentioned as part of the Emblem of a subordinate figure depicted on the Hieroglyphic Stairway at Palenque (Robertson 1985), a figure who may be cited on a hieroglyphic block from Pomona. There is growing evidence that the lords of Palenque, and particularly Chan Bahlum, exercised considerable influence over the Tabasco lowlands; one member of this family may even be recorded at distant Comalcalco.

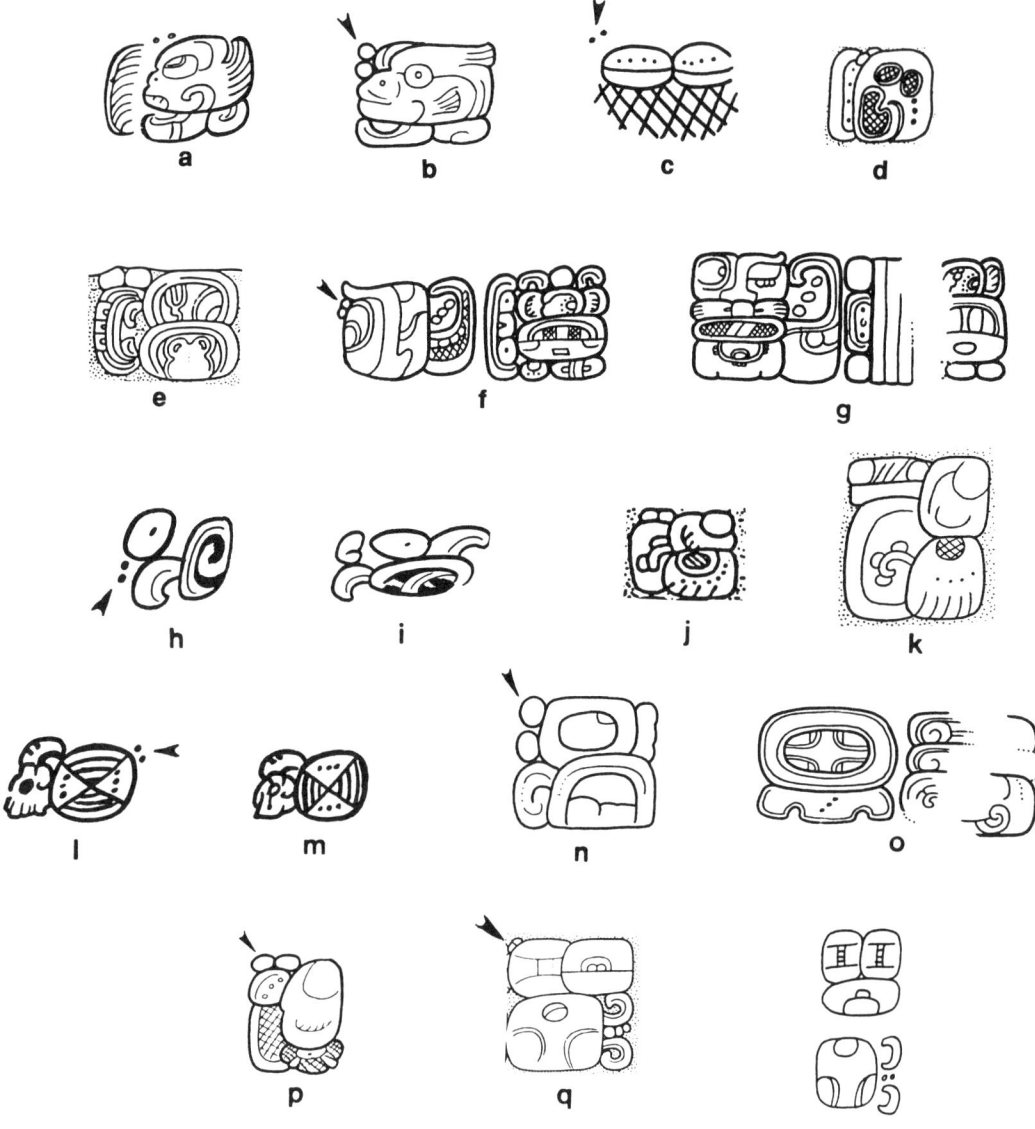

Fig. 57 Doubled phonetic spellings

(a) Rio Azul "chocolate vessel" (Hall et al. 1990: fig. 2)
(b) Piedras Negras Lintel 3: P2 (after photographs by David Stuart)
(c) unprovenanced shell collar (after Kerr photo no. 1874)
(d) Palenque Tablet of the Foliated Cross: M3 (Lounsbury 1980: fig. 2)
(e) Copan Stela 49 (drawing by David Stuart)
(f) Piedras Negras Lintel 3: F2–G1 (after photos by David Stuart)
(g) Pomona Tablet 1: pE5–pF5 (after unpublished drawing by Ian Graham)
(h) unprovenanced vessel (after Kerr photo no. 1092)
(i) unprovenanced vessel (after Kerr photo no. 1092)
(j) Piedras Negras Lintel 2: J2 (after drawing by David Stuart)

(k) glyphic altar, Lacanha area: K1 (after photos supplied by Richard Townsend)
(l) vessel from Tikal Burial 196 (W. Coe 1967: 52)
(m) vessel from Tikal Burial 196 (W. Coe 1967: 52)
(n) panel, Bonampak area: D4 (after unpublished drawing by Ian Graham)
(o) panel, Bonampak area: D4 (after unpublished drawing by Ian Graham)
(p) glyph from unprovenanced panel, B5 (after photos by Nicholas Hellmuth)
(q) Yaxchilan Hieroglyphic Stairway 3: D6 (*CMHI* 3: 166)
(r) Yaxchilan Hieroglyphic Stairway 3: E1–E2 (*CMHI* 3: 166).

Fig. 58 Hieroglyphs from Tikal Stela 31

(a) C6–C7
(b) C11–D11
(c) D16–C17
(d) D26–C27
(e) F14–E15

(f) F26–F27
(g) G5–G6
(h) H21–G24 (all drawings from Jones and
　　　Satterthwaite 1982: fig. 52).

Another verb followed by place names has recently been deciphered by Nikolai Grube and Barbara MacLeod (MacLeod 1990: 339–341; Schele and Freidel 1990: 459). This verb consists of several variants, all of which can be shown to have equivalent, or near-equivalent, readings: T45: 82 (Fig. 59a) // T45: 849: 126 (Fig. 59b) // T713b: 24.181 (Fig. 59c). Grube and MacLeod marshal persuasive evidence that the correct reading is based on a root *hul,* "to arrive," a term of wide distribution in Mayan languages. In addition, one variant—a moon sign containing what appears to be a human eye (Fig. 60a)—is more likely to read **UL,** also "to arrive" in some languages (Barrera Vásquez 1980: 900); this reading seems justified because the sign appears to function as a complement *ul* to *ch'ul,* as in the spelling of **CH'UL-ul,** "holy," at the site of Seibal (Fig. 60b).

The *hul* reading has many interesting implications for Glyph D of the Lunar Series, where it refers to the beginning of the current lunation (MacLeod 1990: 339). But we are concerned here with its function outside that series. At present, there are several texts employing *hul* in nonlunar contexts. In each case, the texts appear to refer to the "arrival" not of the moon, but of a historic figure. One of the best examples is the arrival of "Lady 6 Sky of Dos Pilas," who came to a part of the site of Naranjo at 9.12.10.5.12 (Fig. 61). This event was of great importance to the Naranjo dynasty, for it coincided with the beginning of its resurgence as a dynastic power.

A similar expression occurs on Caracol Stela 3, which records an "arrival" at **OX-WITS-A,** possibly for *Oxwitsha',* "Three Hill Water" (Fig. 62). "Three Hill" is a location attested in several other texts at Caracol, including Stela 10: A4 (Fig. 63a), Stela 15: C12 (Fig. 63b), and Stela 17: C3 (Fig. 63c); several looted vessels may also refer to this place, although their immediate glyphic contexts are still ambiguous. We have seen, too, that "Three Hill" is mentioned in association with the Early Classic ruler K'inich Yax K'uk' Mo'. Whether this is the same place at or near Caracol is impossible to tell.

Of the toponyms at Caracol, those on Stela 3 are among the most intriguing syntactically. One that is preceded by *hul* is followed by an expression reading *y-ila,* "he saw it," and by the name of an individual (Fig. 62). Presumably, the verb indicates that this person "saw" the "arrival" at "Three Hill Water." Quirigua Altar L displays a closely similar pattern in its record of the "arrival" (*hul-ah*) of Smoke-Imix-God K at

**a**

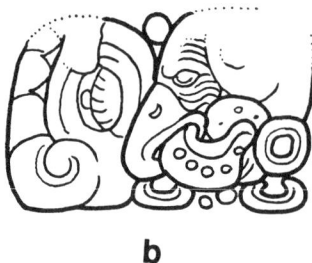
**b**

**c**

Fig. 59 *Hul* verbs

(a) Naj Tunich Group 4m: A3 (drawing by Stephen Houston)

(b) Copan Hieroglyphic Stairway, Step 1: E (drawing by Barbara Fash, courtesy of William Fash, director, Copan Mosaics Project)

(c) Caracol Stela 3: C11 (after Beetz and Satterthwaite 1981: fig. 4).

Fig. 60 The "eye" glyph in various spellings

(a) variant of the lunar series *hul* verb, Yaxchilan
    Lintel 46: D1 (*CMHI* 3: 101)
(b) "eye" sign in Emblem Glyph, Seibal Stela 8: C2
    (after Maler 1908b: pl. 10).

Fig. 61 Arrival of "Lady 6 Sky" at Naranjo, recorded
on Stela 24: C7–C10 (*CMHI* 2: 64).

Fig. 62 Arrival at "Three Hill Water," recorded on
Caracol Stela 3: C11–D12 (after Beetz and
Satterthwaite 1981: fig. 4).

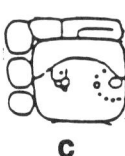

**a**    **b**    **c**

Fig. 63 The "Three Hill" place name

(a) Caracol Stela 10: A4 (after drawing by Stephen Houston, courtesy of Caracol Project)

(b) Caracol Stela 15: C12 (after drawing by Stephen Houston, courtesy of Caracol Project)

(c) Caracol Stela 17: C3 (after drawing by Stephen Houston, courtesy of Caracol Project).

Fig. 64 Quirigua Altar L (Maudslay 1889–1902, 2: pl. 49).

a                                          b

Fig. 65 Arrivals

(a) at Seibal, as recorded on Seibal Stela 11: B1 (after Maler 1908b: pl. 9)

(b) at Dos Pilas, as recorded on Dos Pilas Hieroglyphic Stairway 2: A5b–A6a (after unpublished drawing by Ian Graham).

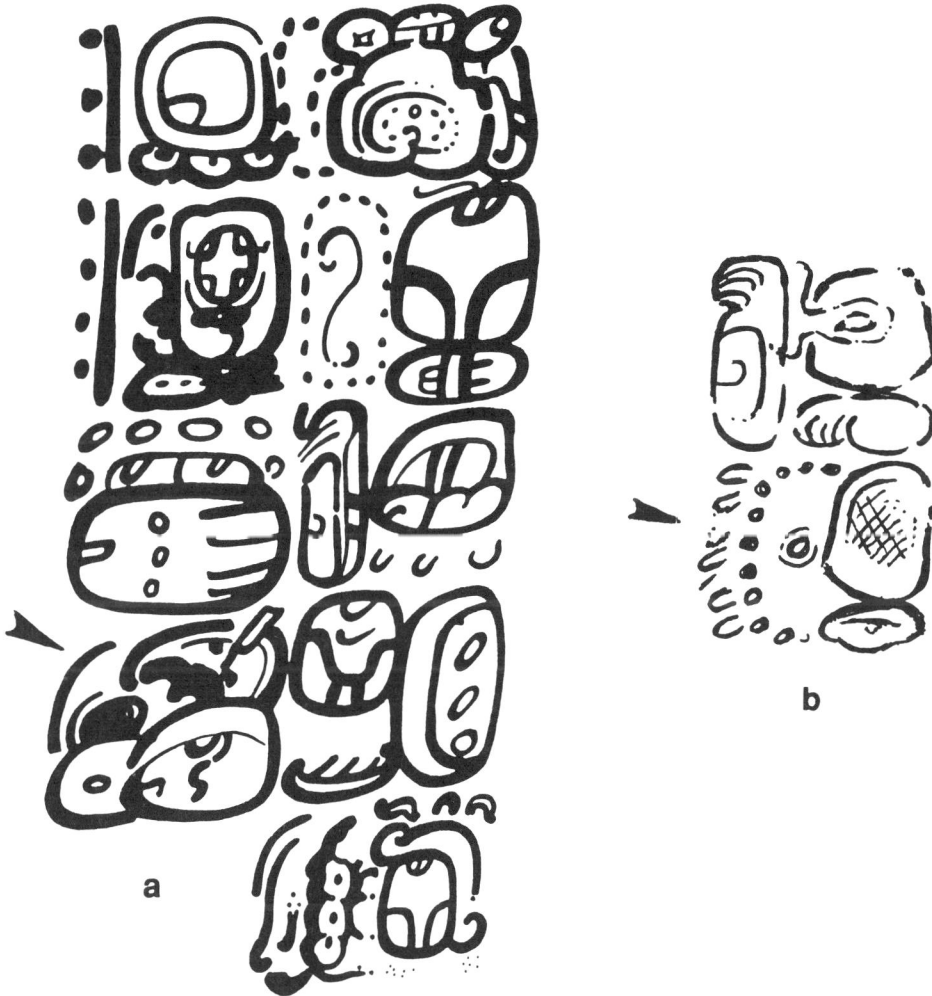

a                                          b

Fig. 66 Place names at Naj Tunich

(a) "arrival event" in Group 4 (after photo courtesy of George Stuart, National Geographic Society)

(b) *ilah mopan* in Group 4h: A3–A4 (after photo courtesy of George Stuart, National Geographic Society).

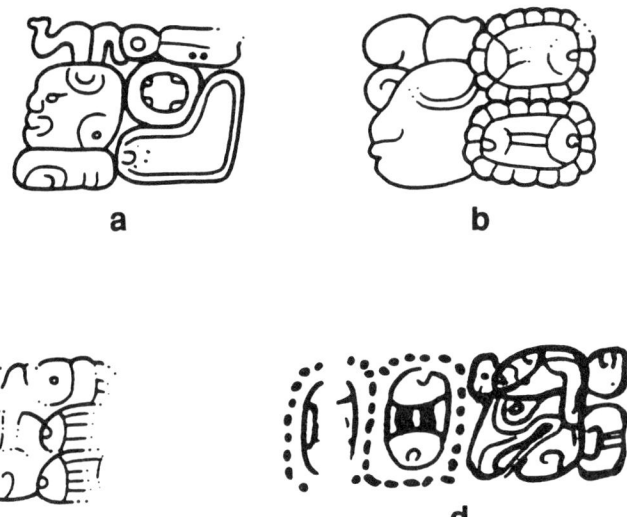

a  b

c  d

Fig. 67 "Smoking head" verbs and place names

(a) the place of Ucanal recorded on Ixkun Stela 2: C9 (after *CMHI* 2: 141)

(b) the "dotted **ko**" place recorded on Naranjo Stela 22: G7 (after *CMHI* 2:56)

(c) the "dotted **ko**" place recorded after a "shell-star" event, Naranjo Stela 18: H9 (after *CMHI* 2: 47)

(d) "dotted **ko**" *ahaw,* recorded on sherd from Buenavista del Cayo, Belize (drawing courtesy of Jennifer Taschek and Joseph Ball).

Quirigua; this event was "seen" by a local figure (Fig. 64), who witnessed the arrival of this visitor from Copan.

"Arrivals" are attested elsewhere as well. Seibal Stela 11 records an arrival at the "Seibal place" (see previous discussion; Fig. 65a), and one text on Dos Pilas Hieroglyphic Stairway 2 documents an arrival at the "Dos Pilas place" (Fig. 65b). Finally, the *hul* expressions in the Naj Tunich cave may refer to arrivals at the cave itself (Fig. 66a); elsewhere, texts in the cave may record the name *Mopan,* possibly in reference to the nearby historical town of the same name (Fig. 66b).

A final verb that is followed by place names is the so-called smoking head, which contains a *k'in* infix and a human profile. The head, which serves as a verb, is clearly war related (Schele 1982: 103–104). What we wish to point out is that the glyphs *after* the event are sometimes recognizable toponyms or toponymic signs. On Ixkun Stela 2, the place name is that of Ucanal, proba-

bly the site that Ixkun warred against (Fig. 67a). Even better examples come from Naranjo, in which a particular site in the vicinity of Naranjo was the subject both of a "smoking head" and a "shell-star" event, both events taking place in the reign of Smoking Squirrel (Figs. 67b–c; Houston, Stuart, and Taube 1992). This "doubled **ko**" place has also been attested on ceramics from western Belize (Fig. 67d), suggesting a location somewhere between Naranjo and the Belizean border, if not into Belize itself.

In summary, Maya script employs place names in all parts of a phrase, both at the end, in toponymic formula, and at the beginning, in ways that specify the location of important events. These expressions amplify considerably our knowledge of Classic toponymy, both by augmenting the number of place names and by indicating the range of events that took place in these locations.

CHAPTER 4

# The Iconography of Place Names

We have mentioned only briefly a strong relationship between our supposed place names and the iconographic images occurring in registers beneath scenes or standing figures. The interplay between text and image in the "Chaak pages" of the Dresden Codex is perhaps the best known example of this relationship (Fig. 1). Similarly, the place glyphs of Aguateca (Fig. 8d), Dos Pilas, and Machaquila have all appeared as iconographic components on which a ruler stands to show his location during an event. The practice is indeed widespread throughout Mesoamerica: the incorporation of place glyphs into iconographic images can be seen in some of the earliest sculptural art of Central Mexico and Oaxaca (e.g., Caso 1928: 34). The fundamental graphic principle for showing location appears with a much more general scope of reference on stelae from the site of Balancan, where lords stand on bands or registers containing **KAB** or "earth" glyphs (Fig. 68; Lizardi Ramos 1961: 121); similar examples appear on Panels 11 and 12 at Dos Pilas (Figs. 69a–b; Navarrete and Luján Muñoz 1963: 36). The convention simply shows what is underfoot, whether it be soil, stone, or "split hills," such as at Aguateca. A look at these lower registers on other monuments should thus lead to the identification of additional place names.

Stela 3 from Yaxha, dating to the Early Classic period, simply illustrates how place can be repre-sented by glyphs below the feet of individuals (Fig. 70). The ruler stands on three glyphs. The first is poorly understood, although it is probably a place name of some sort, and the second is easily recognizable as the Yaxha glyph. This, in turn, is followed by the common "sky-bone" compound. Save the *ut-i* verb, these are the basic components of the place name formula described in Chapter 1. Here, however, the act and actor are portrayed rather than written. The place glyphs function precisely as they would after *ut-i,* but in an iconographic capacity.

Similar iconographic place glyphs can take a very simple form. On Yaxchilan Stela 4, a blood-letting ritual is shown above a basal register consisting of little more than a huge cleft sky sign—the Yaxchilan Emblem Glyph (Fig. 71). A some-what more iconic version occurs on a carved step on Hieroglyphic Stairway 3 (Fig. 72). This sculpture commemorates the capture of a war prisoner by Shield Jaguar on the date 9.12.8.14.1 12 Imix 4 Pop, and later records his accession (Proskouria-koff 1963). The image of the prisoner and the in-scription that surrounds him are placed atop a com-plex iconographic assemblage including the image of the "Cosmic Serpent" and a deity portrait within a thick cartouche. Below the cartouche is a bird head in profile with a cleft at its top. This is the head variant for "sky," therefore again repre-senting the Emblem Glyph main sign of Yaxchilan. Interestingly, in front of the Emblem is T606, read **TAN,** "within." Presumably the image signals that the scene took place "within Yaxchilan." By implication, the "split sky" sign may have been the principal place name of the site.

Yet another example of an iconographic place glyph was recently pointed out to us by Linda Schele and Nikolai Grube (personal communication, 1990). It consists of "**WAK-e-bu-NAL,**" or "*Wakebnal*," the *eb* being spelled with the conflated syllables **e** (T741a) and **bu** (T21v). On Seibal "Stela" 7, a ballplayer stands on the glyph, doubtless because *eb* is a term for Maya stairways (Fig. 73), with which the Classic ballgame was closely connected (Miller and Houston 1987). A reference to a Seibal lord at the site of Anonal displays the name directly after the Seibal Emblem (Fig. 74). Although lacking the *a*, the spelling is suggestive, for it hints at a parallel with titles of origin. In our opinion, "*Wakebnal*" refers to some place within or close to Seibal, perhaps even an actual ballcourt.

Many early monuments from Tikal have complex basal registers that make use of the main sign of the Tikal Emblem Glyph. The newly found Stela 39, for example, shows this sign in a compound placed next to the legs of a captive figure (Fig. 75a). The compound includes a *yax* sign, the Tikal main sign, the sky glyph, and an animal head distinguished by its trilobed eyelid. Interestingly, this grouping of elements also composes part of the inscription on the side of the monument, where the *yax,* Tikal, "sky," and animal glyphs close the text (Fig. 75b). Introducing the signs is an early example of the "chuen-skull" variant of *ut-i,* confirming their functional role as locational glyphs. The example from Stela 39 demonstrates a close link between a supposed place name in the basal register of a monument and its exact counterpart in the inscription; a similar pattern, possibly in reference to some specific location within Tikal, appears in both text and image on Tikal Stela 1 (Fig. 76; Jones and Satterthwaite 1982: fig. 1).

That the "*yax* Tikal" compound refers to Tikal is supported by its appearance in the basal register of Altar 8 of that site (Fig. 77). In a scene reminis-

Fig. 68 Earth signs on Balancan Stela 4 (Lizardi Ramos 1961: 121).

Fig. 69 Dos Pilas panels
(a) Panel 11

(b) Panel 12 (both drawings by Stephen Houston).

59

Fig. 70 Yaxha Stela 3 (after Maler 1908a: pl. 15).

cent of Stela 39, a bound captive lies atop a group of elements that includes *yax,* the Tikal sign, and an eyelidded zoomorph that may be related to the animal sign on Stela 39. The only "missing" component is the sky glyph. Another instance of this cluster of signs is on the bottom of Lintel 2 of Structure 5D–3, where the "sky-bone" glyph is present (Jones and Satterthwaite 1982: 72). In both cases the iconographic evidence points to a toponymic function for the "*yax* Tikal" sign.

At the nearby site of Uolantun we see another iconographic location that may link Classic modes of representing place with much earlier iconographic traditions of Mesoamerica. Although Stela 1 (Fig. 78), an Early Classic monument, is weathered on most of its surface, enough remains of the detail to see the lower register or band upon which the ruler is shown standing. We assume this to be a location reference of some sort. A zoomorphic head occupies the left end of the image and faces outward. Vegetation elements sprouting from the head correspond to the Early Classic forms of the **NAL** sign, suggesting that this may be a place glyph. A bird head occupies the right side of the register, with three distinctive pointed elements emerging from behind

the beak. On the Tikal monuments just discussed, the same tripartite device was seen on owl head variants of the "bone" sign. This bird is most probably the owl with the trilobed eyelid. Between these two heads, in the central area of the register, a sky glyph is clearly visible. Reading all three elements from left to right we see: (a) a place glyph, (b) sky, and (c) the head variant of the bone. Showing the ruler atop a place glyph and "sky-bone," the Uolantun example is very much like that on Yaxha Stela 3. The arrangement of elements is significantly different, however, and may be connected with early examples of place iconography from Preclassic times.

The origins of such place name imagery can be traced not only to the beginnings of monumental art in the Maya lowlands, but also well beyond, to the later Formative and possibly non-Maya monuments of the cultures found at Izapa and at sites farther to the west (Fig. 79). A convention shared by many of these sculptures is the use of a band with a zoomorphic head at each end, a form that is likely to be ancestral to the base registers and bands in Classic Maya art. Excellent examples of such bands occur on Izapa Stelae 1, 22, 23, and 54, which suggest that one of the place names

Fig. 71  Yaxchilan Emblem Glyph, Yaxchilan Stela 4
(preliminary drawing by David Stuart).

Fig. 72 Image from Yaxchilan Hieroglyphic Stairway
3, Step 3 (*CMHI* 3: 169).

Fig. 73 Seibal "Stela" 7 (after Maler 1908b: pl. 5).

Fig. 74 Panel text from Anonal (after photo by Ian Graham).

in use at the site may have been "misty water," at least to judge from the smoke scrolls issuing from what may be a body of water (Figs. 79c–d; Norman 1973: pls. 2,36,38,54); Abaj Takalik Stela 4 has another such watery place name (Porter 1985: figs. 6–8). The bands from Izapa invite comparison with the San Diego cliff carving, a relief in the Maya lowlands that dates to the final years of the Preclassic period (Fig. 80). The sole difference between the Izapa, Abaj Takalik, and San Diego registers seems to be in direction of the zoomorphic heads: the San Diego example faces outward; the Izapa and Abaj Takalik ones, inward. However, in contrast to the bands from the southern lowlands, those from sites on the Pacific piedmont pose a near insuperable obstacle for future investigation: they are unaccompanied by texts and are thus unlikely to be anything other than a subject for conjecture.

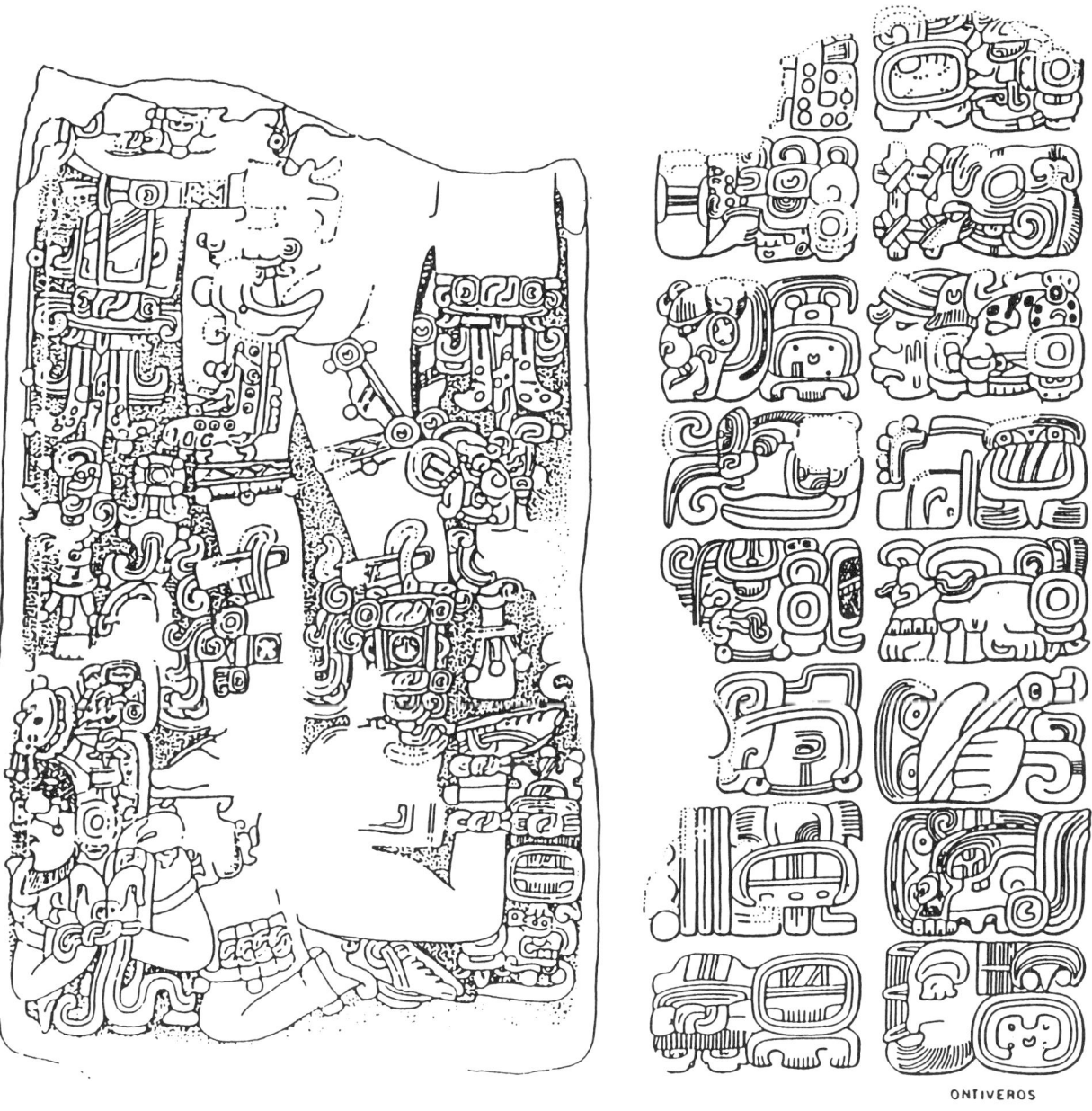

Fig. 75 Tikal Stela 39
(a) front (Ayala Falcón 1987: fig. 2)                    (b) back (Ayala Falcón 1987: fig. 3).

Fig. 77 Tikal Altar 8 (Jones and Satterthwaite 1982: fig. 30).

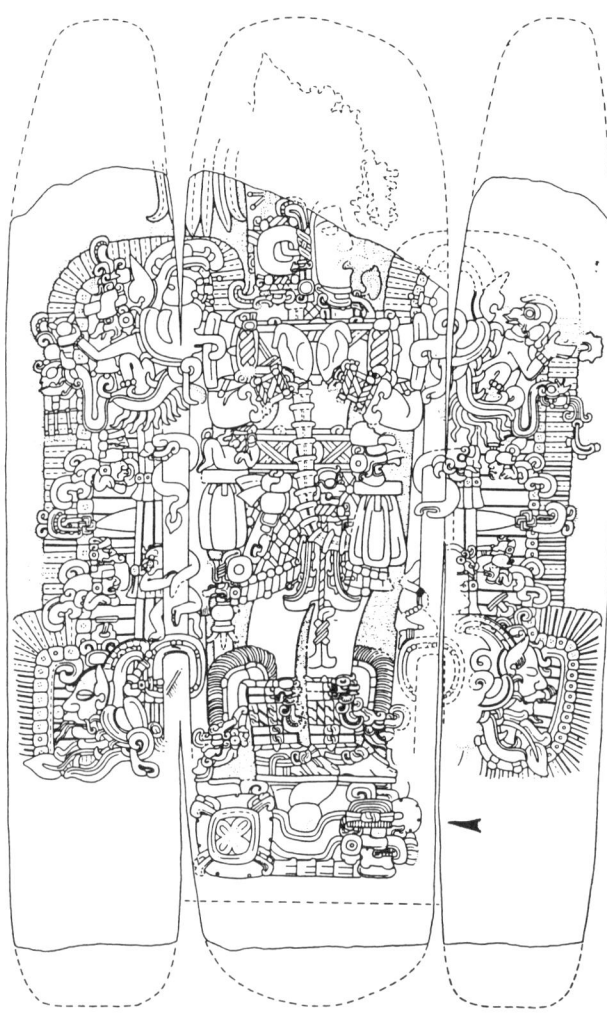

Fig. 76 Tikal Stela 1 (Jones and Satterthwaite 1982: fig. 1).

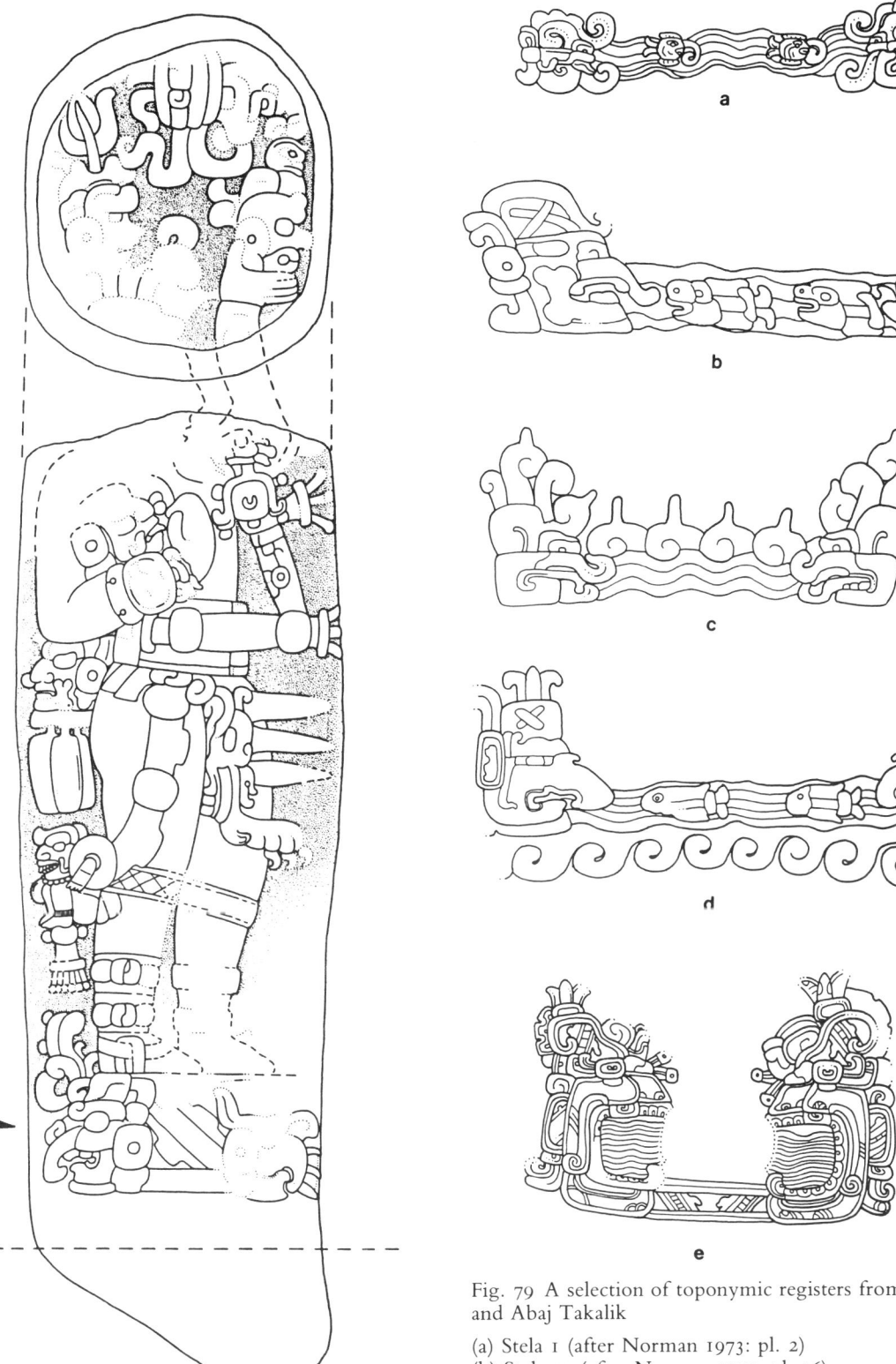

Fig. 78 Uolantun Stela 1 (Jones and Satterthwaite 1982: fig. 76a).

Fig. 79 A selection of toponymic registers from Izapa and Abaj Takalik

(a) Stela 1 (after Norman 1973: pl. 2)
(b) Stela 22 (after Norman 1973: pl. 36)
(c) Stela 23 (after Norman 1973: pl. 38)
(d) Stela 67 (after Norman 1973: pl. 54)
(e) Abaj Takalik Stela 4 (after Porter 1985: fig. 6–8).

Fig. 80 Toponymic register from San Diego cliff carving (after unpublished field drawing by Ian Graham).

CHAPTER 5

# Mythological Place Names

Thus far, the place names under consideration have mostly pertained to historical events and individuals. As we have seen, however, in the "Chaak pages" of the Dresden Codex, place names also appear in texts that treat mythological or supernatural happenings. These can be seen on many examples of Maya art from the Classic period and allow for several new insights into the geography of Maya religious belief.

Our discussion of glyphs that describe the settings of mythical and supernatural events should begin with a closer examination of the tablet of Temple 14 from Palenque. At the beginning of this study, we mentioned the expression *ut-i xaman*, which closes the short descriptive caption of the tablet's scene; it apparently specifies that this event "happened in the north." Other, more precise locations are given in the three hieroglyphs that appear in the bottom register of the scene, amid the water symbols upon which the figures of Chan Bahlum and his mother rest (Fig. 81). The middle glyph is composed of three parts: the head variant of T128 (a locative of some sort?), the smoke sign read either *k'ak'* or *buts'* (depending on context), and the sign *nab*. We read the final two components as **K'AK'-NAB,** for *k'ak'nab,* "ocean." The **K'AK'-NAB** combination occurs without the T128 prefix on the Palace Tablet from Palenque (at block D5). The "ocean" reading accords with the surrounding water sym-

bolism, as well as with the **na** and **ba** signs in the lowest register that seem to spell *nab,* "lake, pool, body of water" (Linda Schele, personal communication, 1978). The first of the three glyphs amid the water symbols remains undeciphered, though it may include the combination **HO-NIK-TE** for *ho nikte',* "five flowers." The third of the glyphs in the basal register is perhaps also locational, for it occurs in the main text of the tablet after *ut-i* and after a sentence that restates the caption of the scene. This locational sign stands in place of the *xaman,* "north," glyph albeit with a different reading (**SAK-?-NAL**). Its use here illustrates neatly the complementary association between place names in iconography and text.

One of the more frequent locations mentioned in mythological texts is illustrated in Figure 82. This place is linked consistently with events that occurred at the beginning of the current Baktun cycle, at 13.0.0.0.0 4 Ahau 8 Cumku. The components are consistent in all known examples: T128 (in either its conventional or head form) with "sky," followed by a compound made up of **YAX,** a "triple cauac" main sign (identical to that of the Seibal Emblem Glyph), and the **-NAL** superfix. The location is mentioned on the Tablets of the Cross and Sun at Palenque (Figs. 82a–b), the text of Stela 12 at Copan (Fig. 82c), Stela C of Quirigua (Fig. 82d), where it follows *ut-i;* it also occurs on the inscribed Altar 1 from Piedras Ne-

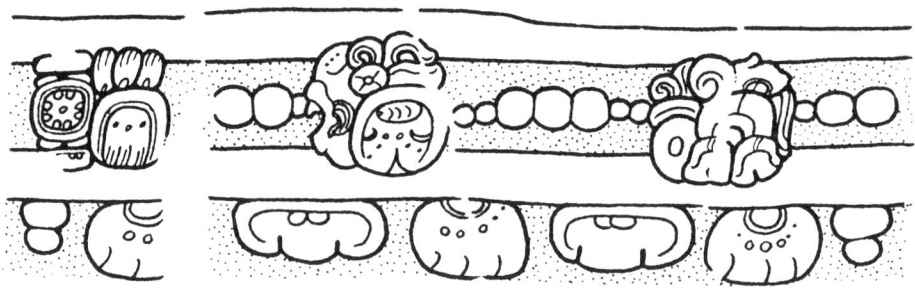

Fig. 81 Toponymic hieroglyphs from basal register of Temple 14 tablet, Palenque (after Schele 1988: fig. 10.4).

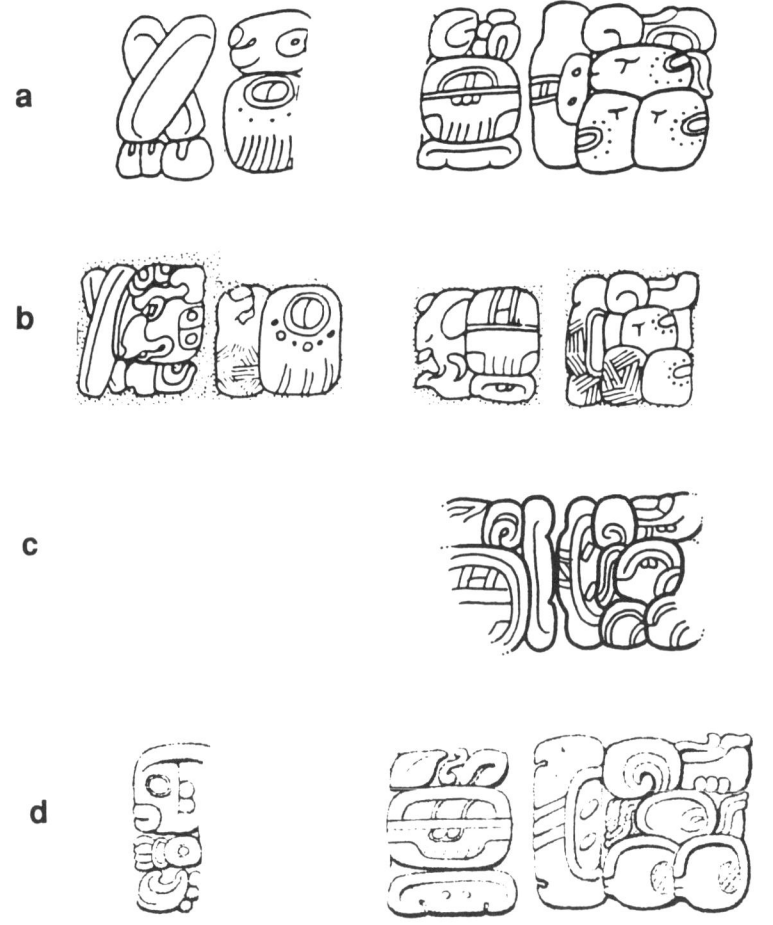

Fig. 82 Place names associated with the beginning of the current Maya era

(a) Palenque Tablet of the Cross: C6b–C7 (drawing by Linda Schele, in Lounsbury 1980: fig. 1)

(b) Palenque Tablet of the Sun: D16–N2 (drawing by Linda Schele, in Lounsbury 1980: fig. 3)

(c) Copan Stela 12, south side: A14 (drawing by David Stuart)

(d) Quirigua Stela C: B13–A14 (after Maudslay 1889–1902: pl. 19).

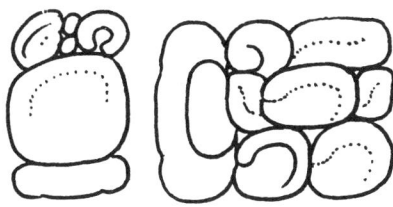

Fig. 83 Another "era" place name from Piedras Negras Altar 1 (drawing by David Stuart).

gras (Fig. 83). In all cases the texts refer to the place of events that happened at 13.0.0.0.0. The Quirigua example is the most explicit in this regard, for it names this place as the spot where some mythic personage dedicated a monument. Yet another reference appears on Stela 12 from Copan, but there the inscription is damaged and the context unclear.

The inscriptions of Quirigua contain perhaps the largest collection of mythological place names. Most signs are rare, if not unique, and reveal little of their meaning. Yet at least one toponym appears in several contexts and is thus somewhat easier to interpret. Figure 84 illustrates the compound, which includes three signs, T4: V: 561, or **NA-HO-KAAN,** "First Five Sky(?)" (Houston 1984: 797, 799). With the addition of *ahaw,* the reading becomes *Nahokaan Ahaw* ("lord[s] of *Nahokaan*") and serves as the epithet of the pair of deities named the "Paddlers" (Mathews n.d.c; Stuart 1984, 1988a). As a title, it serves notice that the Paddlers were lords of a particular place in Maya mythic geography. Without the *ahaw* glyph, it functions simply as a place name.

Quirigua Stela C (position A9b) provides a good example of the pattern in that it connects the *Nahokaan* compound with the names of the Paddlers at 13.0.0.0.0 4 Ahau 8 Cumku, the beginning of the current era (Fig. 84a). Additional

evidence comes from the site of Tonina, Mexico, where there occur many examples of the place glyph as a title of the Paddlers. Another version of the *Nahokaan* glyph appears on an unprovenanced vessel (Fig. 84b), where it follows *ut-i* and precedes the signs for *wits* and "north." This phrase may be an elaboration on the place reference, to which the scribes have supplied additional, geographic information. In the accompanying scene, the Paddlers sit upon entwined serpents (Robicsek and Hales 1981: 20b). The mythological nature of *Nahokaan* is reinforced by its association with GII of the Palenque Triad (Berlin 1963): on the jamb inscription from the inner sanctuary of the Temple of the Foliated Cross, GII—the infant God K—is also termed the *Nahokaan Ahaw,* or "fifth sky lord" (Fig. 84c).

Another place glyph linked with mythological settings is shown in Figure 85. Its main sign, T769, probably refers to a depression or hole, with which it appears on page 43a of the Dresden Codex (Fig. 85d; Thompson 1972). Of the two affixes, one is T86, **-NAL;** the other, the sign for "black." On Dresden page 43a, as elsewhere, black is associated with "west." A similar concern with directions appears on the base of the panel from Temple 14 at Palenque, where a mythological place name is linked with the color "white" and the direction "north" (see previous discussion).

What is the significance of the glyph with "black?" Following Peter Mathews (personal communication, 1983), we believe its meaning may have been something like "black hole," a feature serving as the apparent locus of ballplaying in mythological time, as on Yaxchilan Hieroglyphic Stairway 2, Step 7, at G5 (Fig. 85a). We should note, however, that, when coupled with the *ahaw* title, it can also appear as a name glyph of Classic period lords (Fig. 85b).[15] And one example from Lacanha appears after an *ut-i* expression (Fig. 85c), in inexplicable associa-

---

[15] In the Popol Vuh, as well as among the living Quiche Maya, there is a strong association between ballcourts and the underworld, with the former being viewed as entrances to the latter (Tedlock 1985: 46). The cave images of Naj Tunich (G.

Stuart 1981), where ballplaying is depicted, point to similar conclusions. That a ballgame would be played at "black hole," a dark subterranean place, is consistent with this notion.

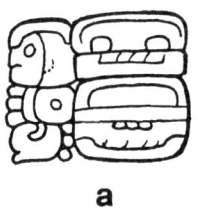

a

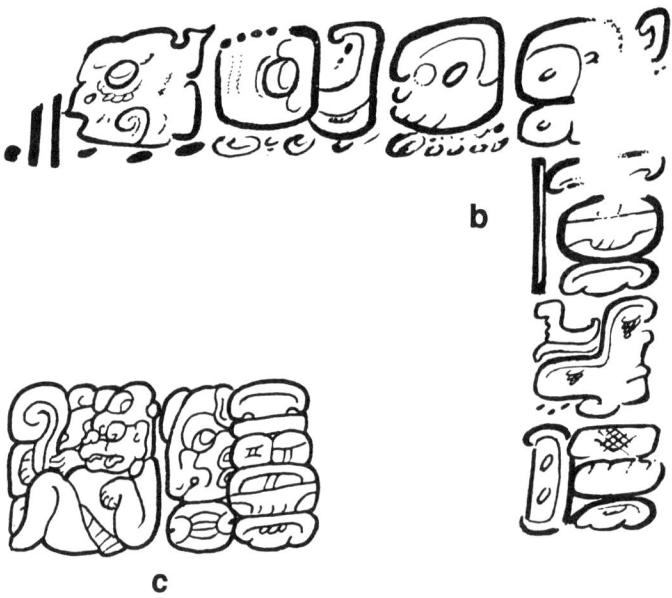

b

c

Fig. 84 "Fifth sky" place names

(a) Quirigua Stela C: A9 (after Maudslay 1889–1902: pl. 19)

(b) unprovenanced vessel (after Kerr 1989: 36)

(c) Palenque Temple of the Foliated Cross, Doorjamb: A9–B9 (unpublished drawing by Linda Schele).

tion with a "birth" event that we presume to be mythological in character.

The "black hole" compound is occasionally coupled with a glyph designating a watery environment, T95.86: 522v, which also takes the "black" affix (Fig. 86a). Both are found on the surface of a dish showing supernatural beings in an aquatic setting (Fig. 86b). The representation of the water displays repeating examples of the same place glyph, with the "black" prefix here omitted and indicated instead by the darkened interior of the main sign. Interestingly, the same glyph is also

attested among the large glyphs carved on the exterior of Copan Structure 22A, which has yielded a number of place signs that may be mythical (Fig. 86c). (The building at Copan has been identified as a community house, or *popol nah,* to which members of the nobility, each from the location on which they are seated, repaired to discuss issues of collective interest [Fash et al. 1992]. This is a useful hypothesis, yet, at the same time, difficult to reconcile with the mythological nature of the identifiable signs.)

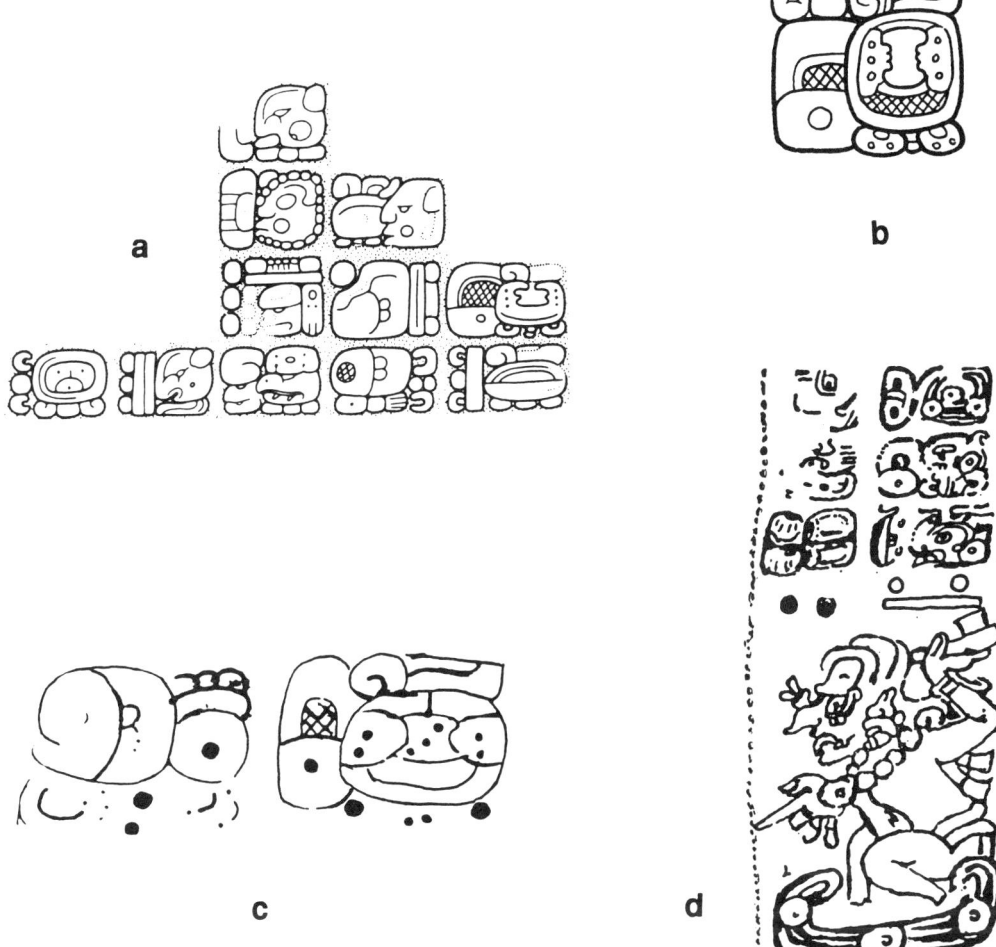

Fig. 85 The "black hole" place name

(a) Yaxchilan Hieroglyphic Stairway 2: C6–G6 (*CMHI* 3: 160)
(b) Quirigua Stela A: C9 (after Maudslay 1889–1902: pl. 7)

(c) Lacanha Panel 1: M5–N5 (after Coe and Benson 1966: fig. 10–11)
(d) Dresden Page 43a (after Villacorta and Villacorta 1930).

Another watery locale is named on the vessel illustrated in Figure 87. Here the combination **UUK-HA-NAL** follows the verb *ut-i* and accompanies a scene of eight individuals in chest-high water. The text describes the scene by providing a date and a verb associated with death, together with the *ut-i* place name formula, which presumably specifies where the subject died. The presence on the vessel of Hunahpu—a figure often depicted in the underworld—suggests that *Uukha'nal* is both mythical and chthonic. As F. Robicsek and D. Hales note, the watery scene is repeated on other vessels in the "codex style," and at least one vessel has the *Uukha'nal* glyph painted on its underside (Robicsek and Hales 1981: 67). It is tempting to see such a placement as the functional equivalent of locational glyphs found on the basal registers of stone monuments, as described in the last chapter.

One mythological toponym appears almost exclusively at Palenque (Fig. 88), with two, rare occurrences at Piedras Negras and an unidentified site, respectively. It is, however, very different in composition from the historic toponym of the site (see Fig. 32). The compound includes T74:

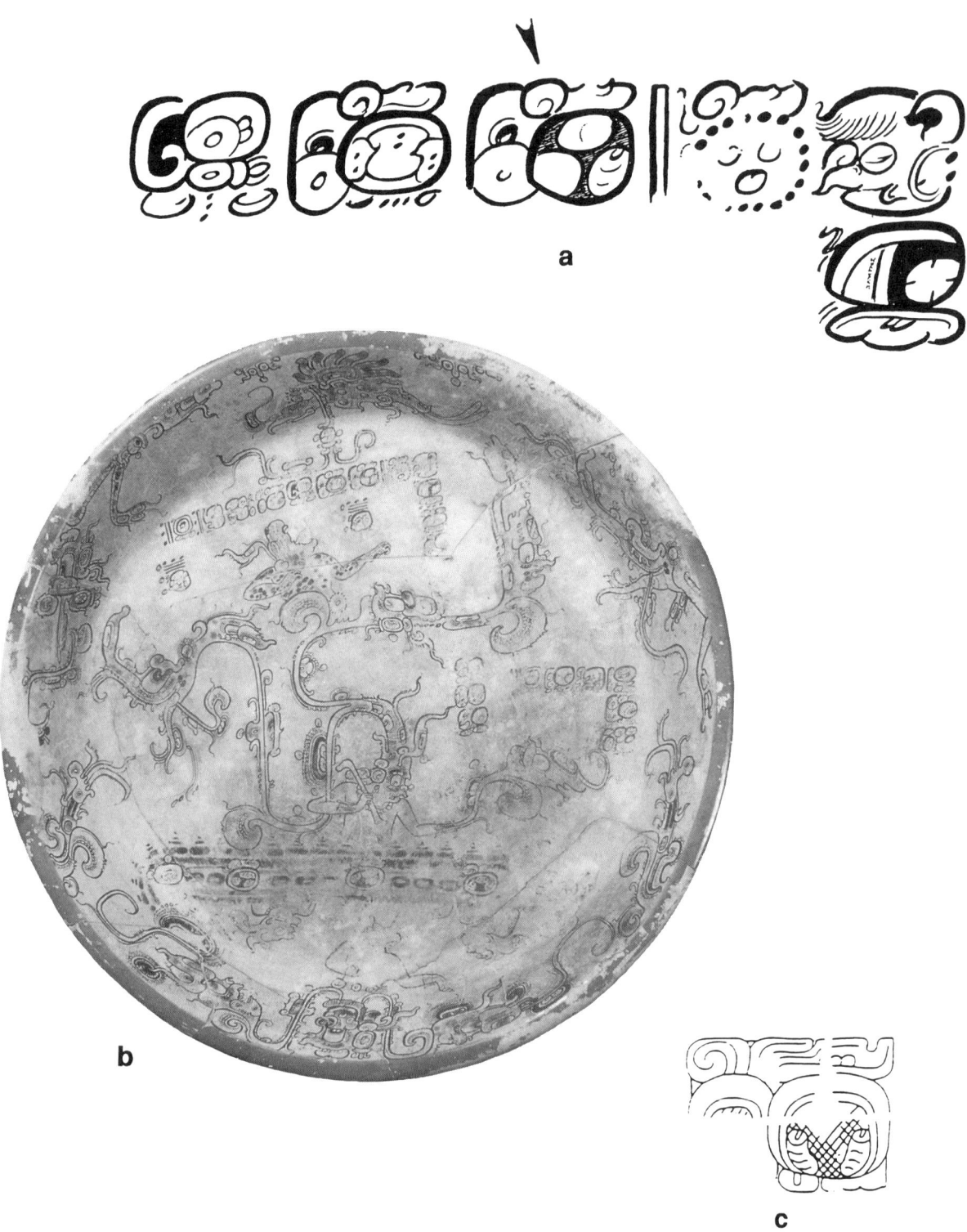

Fig. 86 The "black water" place name

(a) glyphs from unprovenanced "codex-style" dish
    (after Schele and Miller 1986: pl. 122)
(b) overall view of unprovenanced "codex-style" dish
    (photo by Justin Kerr)

(c) "black water" glyph from the facade of Temple
    22A, Copan (drawing by Barbara Fash, courtesy
    of Copan Mosaics Project).

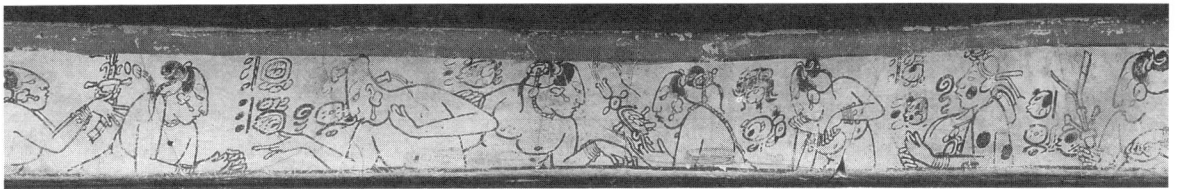

Fig. 87 Watery location (after Robicsek and Hales 1981: 67).

a

b

Fig. 88 *Matawil* place glyphs

(a) Palenque Temple of the Foliated Cross, Alfarda: B2 (drawing by Linda Schele in Lounsbury 1980: fig. 5)

(b) *Matawil* used in Emblem Glyph on the Tablet of the Foliated Cross, Palenque: C11 (drawing by Linda Schele in Lounsbury 1980: fig. 2).

565.117: 178, **ma-ta-wi-la,** or *Matawil*. David Stuart (1978: 171) has already noted the connection between this compound and deities or deceased ancestors, but we are now able to revise some of his general interpretations. Our present opinion is that the glyph is much like the variable element at Seibal, which serves both as toponym and the main sign of the local Emblem Glyph. Evidence from the Tablet of the Temple of the Foliated Cross (C11–D12) indicates that the presence of the lordly titles, such as the "water group" and *ahaw* epithets, transformed the compound into an Emblem Glyph of deities (Fig. 88b). Conversely, it functioned as a toponym in

the absence of such affixation. Similar shifts between title and toponym mark the use of the "black hole" compound (see Fig. 85b).

The *Matawil* glyph occurs rarely outside the Palenque inscriptions. One revealing appearance is on a carved lintel from the region of Yaxchilan, perhaps more specifically from the largely unexplored site of La Pasadita (Fig. 89). The sculpture depicts two individuals, one of whom is drilling fire, possibly as part of a divination ritual. The inscription confirms this, stating that the event was *hoch'ah k'ak'*, or "he drilled the fire." Below the scene of seated figures, a gaping skeletal serpent mouth flanks a short text of six glyphs, which

Fig. 89 *Matawil* depicted on looted panel (after photo, courtesy of Linda Schele).

Fig. 90 *Matawil* in birth expressions, Palenque Temple of the Foliated Cross, Alfarda: A1–C1 (drawing by Linda Schele in Lounsbury 1980: fig. 5).

probably continue from the main inscription above. This glyph panel names a subsidiary lord, or *sahal*, and ends with the glyph **ma-ta-wi**. Although its placement seems odd, we suggest that this refers to *Matawil*, depicted symbolically on this lintel by the skeletal mouth, a common mode for representing the underworld.

Earlier we mentioned the apparent practice of attaching toponyms to verbs as a means of specifying the location of an event. The *Matawil* place name behaves in the same way. In several texts, particularly those related to the births of deities (Lounsbury 1980: 112), the *Matawil* compound follows a birth event, after which occurs the name of the deity born on that day (Fig. 90). In addition, most of the birth verbs include an earth sign, which is "touched" by a human hand, in probable allusion to a metaphor still used by the Chol Maya (Lounsbury 1980: 113). Very likely, *Matawil* is where the deities were born, that is, where they "touched the earth."[16] In some cases, the place name follows a conventional "birth" glyph, a pattern that recalls verb-location phrasing.

But where was *Matawil?* There are hints from the unprovenanced lintel (see Fig. 89), thought by Linda Schele to come from Laxtunich or perhaps La Pasadita (Lamb and Lamb 1951), that *Matawil* corresponded to an area both enclosed and defined by skeletal jaws, such as those into which Pacal falls on the sarcophagus lid at Palenque (Fig. 91). Moreover, we suspect that the pattern of place name usage at Palenque recounts a unique instance from the Classic period of a "migration" legend, a relatively common form of tale in Mesoamerica that charts the history of a people in terms of movements over a landscape fusing real and mythological geography. At Palenque, the earliest (indeed mythical) history takes place in *Matawil,* shifts during the Early Classic period to *Toktan,* and then moves to the *Lakamha'* place mentioned in connection with Late Classic events.

A final mythological place name is one that appears with the "black hole, black water" toponyms on the so-called Cosmic Plate (Fig. 92a). It comprises three signs: the number five, T538 (possibly representing a flower of some sort), and **NAL**. The inscription of Copan Stela C apparently locates this place in the remote, mythological past (Fig. 92c), an association consistent with its appearance on the "Cosmic Plate." The same location may be depicted both glyphically and iconographically on an unprovenanced vessel dating to the Early Classic period (Fig. 93). The text informs us that the name of the drinking vessel (A2–B2, *u k'aba yuch'ib;* Houston, Stuart, and Taube 1989) was the **HO**-T538-**NAL**. The reference is further clarified by the addition afterwards of a skeletal bird head (B1), which, as discussed in Chapter 1, alternates with the so-called bone sign of the sky-bone compound. The location is represented on the sides of the vessel by a head variant of the **WITS**, or "hill," sign; inside a cleft in the hill are two unidentifiable objects. Thus, the name of the vessel is the same as that of

---

[16] One birth expression, that from the Temple of the Cross alfarda, does not conform to the pattern: in this case the deity name appears before the *Matawil* glyph. Nonetheless, this example is anomalous and may simply be a "marked" expression, which departs from unmarked phrasing for enhanced poetic effect.

Fig. 91 Palenque Temple of the Inscriptions,
sarcophagus lid (Robertson 1983: fig. 99).

**a**

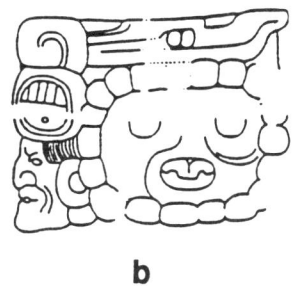
**b**

**c**

Fig. 92 Mythological place name

(a) unprovenanced "codex-style" vessel (after Schele and Miller 1986: pl. 122)
(b) glyph from facade of Temple 22a, Copan (drawing by Barbara Fash, courtesy of Copan Mosaics Project)
(c) Copan Stela C: A10–B10 (after drawing by Barbara Fash, courtesy of Copan Mosaics Project).

a mythological location. That vessels had personal names accords neatly with evidence for name designations of stelae and altars.

Moving away from the Classic period, one of the most fascinating contexts of mythological place glyphs is found in the Postclassic murals from Santa Rita, Belize. Thomas Gann (1900) made excellent copies of these paintings before they were destroyed, and in his renderings we find several of the place glyphs discussed so far in association with complex figures of Maya deities (Fig. 94). The wall painting can be divided into several discrete scenes each involving two or more supernaturals. Above the figures, some of whom are

Fig. 93 Vessel showing mythological place name (after drawing and photograph supplied by Donald Hales).

bound with ropes that are held by their companions, we find isolated glyphs, usually a date ("1 Ahau," "9 Ahau," etc.) and a place glyph. These places include **UUK-HA-NAL,** the "6-Yax-Hand" glyph, and the "legs" glyph, which is identical to an example from Palenque. Probably the places and date glyphs refer to the locations and times for the pictured events. Because all of the dates are simple Ahau signs with coefficients, it has been suggested that these dates may correlate with katun endings in the Maya calendar. We agree with this interpretation and suggest further that the place glyphs tell where the katuns were "established," much in the way locations are emphasized in the katun pages of the Books of Chilam Balam. Unlike the Yucatec historical chronicles, however, these places do not seem to have been historical, in which case the Santa Rita murals present us with a mythological landscape for the katun cycle. It is of interest that militarism is a pervasive theme of these murals. The bound captives, the arrows piercing the ground, and the Xiuhcoatl figure all attest to a belligerent theme to the painting. Perhaps the artists were alluding through a visual pun to one of the important meanings for *k'atun* in Yucatec Maya: "war, battle."

In summary, just as the deities acceded to high office or gave birth, so too did they live in specific places, ranging from the "fifth sky" to the "black hole." Yet the parallels with the lives of Classic Maya lords stop there. On present evidence, the overlap between human and mythological geography would seem to be small: to our knowledge—and excepting the unclear reference at the unidentified site near Yaxchilan—the only certain example is the possible juxtaposition of the Copan place name with the "hole, water" glyphs on Copan Stela 10. And there the affixation of the mythological place signs differs from other occurrences. In general, then, humans did not perform events in the places of supernaturals; nor, apparently, did deities dwell among the Classic Maya. In conceptual terms, their respective geographies were kept rigidly apart. But this does not mean that mythological places were wholly fictitious or imagined. As among the modern Quiche Maya, they might simply have taken the form of distant hills on the horizon, of places regarded as the abode of supernaturals and only rarely visited by humans (Dennis Tedlock, personal communication, 1988).

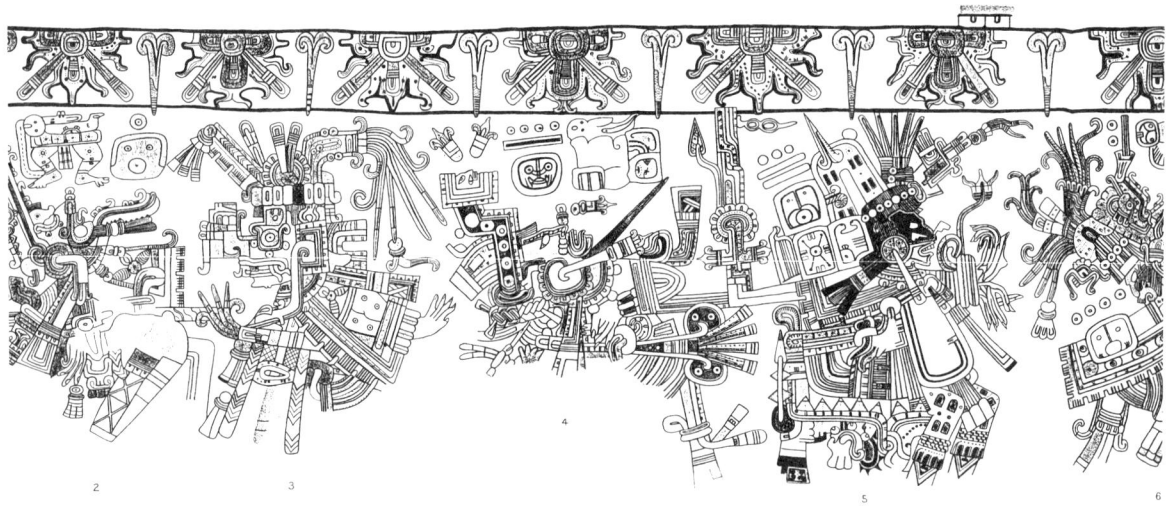

Fig. 94 Santa Rita murals (Gann 1900: pl. XXIX).

CHAPTER 6

# Site Areas and Buildings

We have referred in passing to possible names of places within sites, such as buildings or building groups. In this section we expand briefly on this subject by pointing out other examples of more "specialized" place names and by summarizing present knowledge of how buildings were named by the Classic Maya. The identifications are based on the presence of place name glyphs after verbs, a pattern that throws light not only on the names of sites, but of areas within them. By studying such terms, epigraphers can identify by name certain precincts and buildings of Maya cities, as well as plot the ritual circuits by Maya rulers as they moved from one part of a center to another. Some of these names have already been documented by David Stuart, who has recognized the epithets of building through his studies of dedication rites.

The first example is a mountain place glyph, which Piedras Negras Lintel 3 records as the burial location of Ruler 4 (Fig. 49b). The glyph has the number five followed by the "propeller shield" sign, familiar to many as a part of the name glyph of the famous Palenque ruler Pacal. In fact, it is not a shield, since **PAKAL** is a very different sign that always follows in his name. Instead, the sign in question probably represents a type of flower, and was read **HANAB,** the meaning of which is elusive (Pacal's name therefore is more correctly "Hanab Pacal"). We can fairly eas-

ily read the place as **HO-HANAB-WITS** or, *Hohanabwits*. It is possible that the glyph refers generally to Piedras Negras; however, there is already an acceptable candidate for this sign (see Chap. 2). A stronger explanation is that *Hohanabwits* corresponds to a building within Piedras Negras, and perhaps to the very building that entombs Ruler 4. The key glyph may be the *wits* compound, which serves to distinguish it from the mythological location discussed before. Many of the place names with this glyph may allude not so much to sites, as to specific buildings. The analogy of structure to "hill" accords with ethnographic accounts from the Tzotzil Maya, who link the spirits of ancestors with mountains (Vogt 1976).

The verb-place name pattern is also attested at Tikal, in the inscriptions of katun-ending monuments in the Twin-pyramid complexes (Fig. 95). The structure of these texts is highly regular, inasmuch as each opens with a katun-ending date and a "*tun*-over-hand" verb, doubtless recording the dedication of the *tun,* or stela (Justeson and Mathews 1983). Yet what follows the "*tun*-over-hand" verb and precedes the name of the ruler differs from text to text. It is precisely this variable element that merits closer attention, for we suspect it expresses where an event took place within the overall site of Tikal.

The argument has important implications, in

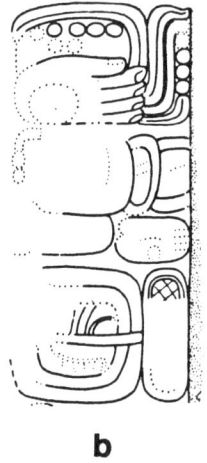

a                              b                              c

Fig. 95 Place names from Twin-pyramid stelae

(a) Stela 16: B1–B2 (Jones and Satterthwaite 1982: fig. 22)
(b) Stela 20: A4–A7 (Jones and Satterthwaite 1982: fig. 29)

(c) Stela 22: B2–A3 (Jones and Satterthwaite 1982: fig. 33).

that it constitutes evidence for glyphic labeling of parts of sites. In the Twin-pyramid inscriptions, for example, the variable elements contain the *wits,* "hill, mountain," glyph. In our opinion, the reference is to hills, but of a special sort: those constructed by humans.

Throughout Mesoamerica, architecture could stand in metaphoric relationship to mountains, as was especially the case among the Aztec (e.g., Broda 1987; Townsend 1982). This was no less true of the ancient Maya. For example, the architectural symbolism of buildings, such as Temple 22 at Copan, reveals that they were regarded as artificial *witsob,* or mountains (personal observation, 1986). **WITS** logographs, one stacked on top of the other, decorate the corners and facades of the building; in this iconographic setting, the doorway of the building is tantamount to a cave. A sculpture from Tonina, Monument 106, contains a more explicit example showing a ruler seated atop the image of a *wits;* the text informs us that the ruler was "seated on the hill," *chum-? t-u wits-il* (Fig. 96). Accordingly, the mountain references at Tikal may well allude to the architec-

tural complex associated with the dedication stelae. And as a result, the Twin-pyramid complexes may now be identified as the "X-hills," the X being the element that differentiates one complex from the other.

Apart from the Twin-pyramid complexes, a monument found in the center of the site may specify other locations at Tikal. This sculpture is Stela 31, which records, among other things, a "*tun*-over-hand" event that took place at 8.18. 0.0.0. The next two glyphs locate this event at "**UUK**-Black-*K'AN*" and "Smoke Mountain" (Fig. 97). The text then tells us that the event celebrated the completion of the eighteenth katun and that the rite occurred "in the land (?)" of Curl Nose, one of the rulers of Tikal. The pattern is the same as that on the Late Classic monuments at Tikal, since "Smoke Mountain" was probably the setting for the Period Ending.

One of the stelae at Tikal is likely to be the stone erected on this date. This is Stela 18, with a probable date of 8.18.0.0.0 (Fig. 98). The monument was recovered from the front of Structure 5D–34–1st, where it had probably been reset

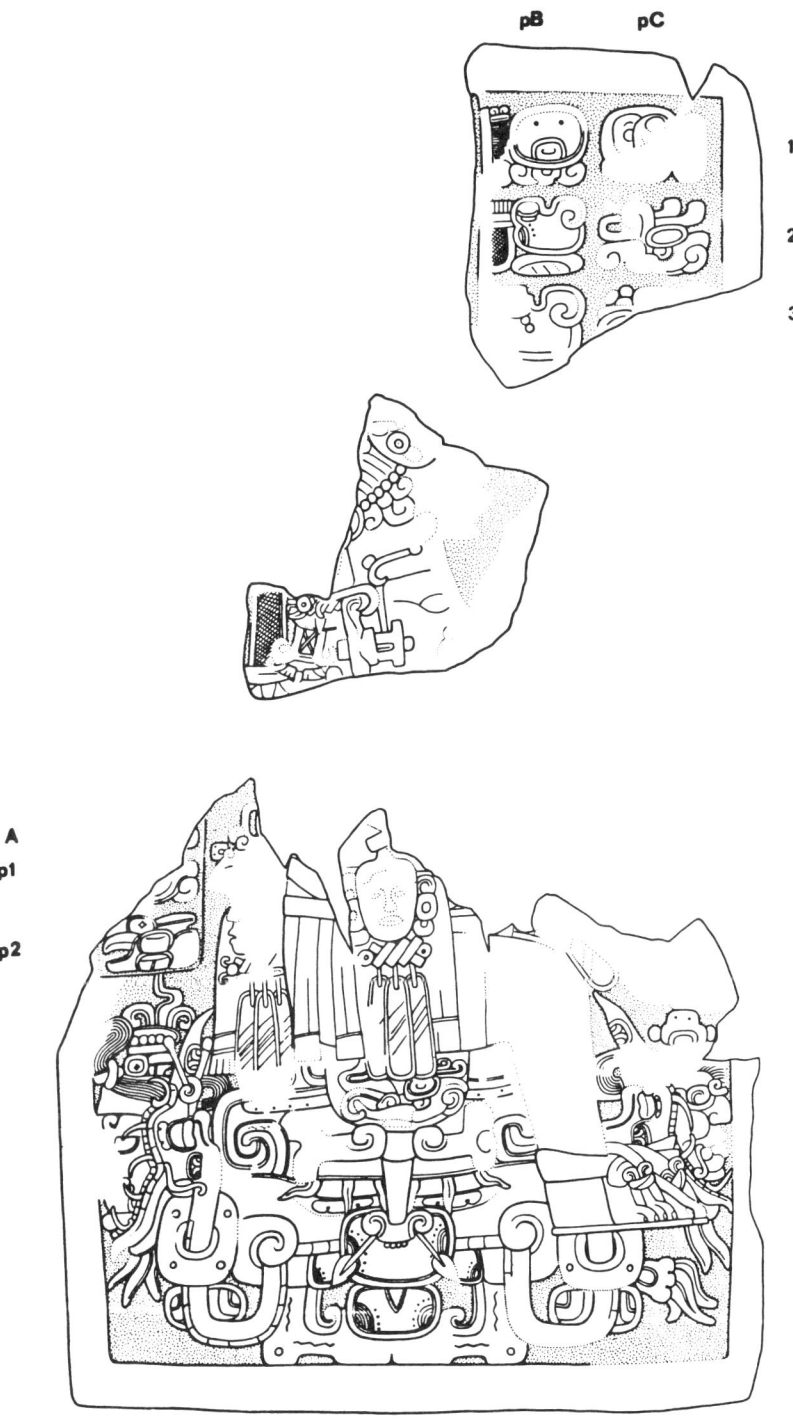

Fig. 96 Tonina Monument 106 (after Becquelin and Baudez 1982: fig. 175).

Fig. 97 Hieroglyphs from Tikal Stela 31: E16–E20 (Jones and Satterthwaite 1982: fig. 52).

from some other location. The only surviving fragment of its front shows a ruler sitting on a mountain (a variant of the "cauac monster"), with a "smoke" sign attached to its forehead. The glyphs parallel neatly the "Smoke Mountain" associated with this date on Stela 31. Perhaps "Smoke Mountain" was a specific location and possibly a building within Tikal.

Another way the scribe(s) of Stela 31 referred to the location of such ceremonies was with the "chuen-skull" expression. We have already suggested that the glyphs following the "chuen-skull" glyph refer to specific locations (see previous discussion). In the absence of a firm reading of the sign, this interpretation remains tentative. Yet, to speculate, the "chuen-skull" may signal the existence of a long list of locations, many probably (although not certainly) within the site of Tikal (see

Fig. 58). If correctly identified, these place names clash with earlier interpretations of them, such as Peter Mathews' identification of one sign as a personal name (Mathews 1985). In an interesting pattern, the verb-with-location and the "chuen-skull" expressions appear to be mutually exclusive, indicating, perhaps, that scribes had at least two ways of conveying information about location.

Another possible reference to an area of a site is found at Palenque (Fig. 32). The place name of Palenque, *Lakamha'*, has already been described. In two instances, the toponym is modified by a series of glyphs, discussed in Chapter 2, including a glyph with the syllables **ye-ma-la,** the head of a quetzal bird (presumably read **K'UK'**), the **LAKAM** sign, and finally the syllabic combination **wi-tsi** for *wits* ("hill, mountain"). This combination, which possibly reads *Yemalk'uk' Lakamwits,* "Descending Quetzal Big Hill," occurs solely in the Cross Group inscriptions and in Temple 18 (Figs. 99a–b). Thus, the mountain may simply be the raised area upon which the Cross Group, Temple 18, and related structures were built (see also the Tablet of the Temple of the Sun, D15–N16, in Lounsbury 1980: fig. 3). Another possibility is that these more specific place glyphs refer to the large hill looming behind the Cross Group.

The clearest evidence of "intrasite" references comes from Dos Pilas. The Dos Pilas place sign (see above) is not the only one in the area, for others appear after *"tun*-over-hand" verbs at the site. On Stelae 14 (9.14.0.0.0; Fig. 100) and 15 (9.14.10.4.0; Fig. 101), for example, one glyph includes the **-NAL** sign and a zoomorphic head with a **K'IN** sign in its forehead; the reading may be *K'inalha',* "warm or hot water." In each instance it precedes the name of the ruler, a structure precisely like that on the texts from the Twin-pyramid complexes, in which the toponym follows a verb and precedes a lord's name. What is doubly interesting is that both Stelae 14 and 15 lie in an outlying "El Duende" group, about 1 km east of the main plaza of Dos Pilas. We strongly suspect that *K'inalha'* names the El Duende outlier, just as, perhaps, the Dos Pilas place sign corresponds to the main plaza.

Fig. 98 Tikal Stela 18 (Jones and Satterthwaite 1982: fig. 26a).

Evidence that might confirm the identification comes from Stela 15. The monument depicts Dos Pilas Ruler 2 (Houston and Mathews 1985), who

stands on the *K'inalha'* glyph. The resemblance to other basal registers is sufficient to suggest that Dos Pilas is portrayed at El Duende, rather than some other part of the site. And where exactly was *K'inalha'*? Approximately 250 m north of the El Duende group issues one of the few springs in this sector of Dos Pilas. The axis of the terraces and main pyramid of El Duende are almost precisely in alignment with this feature (Fig. 102). It is possible that the toponym referred to the spring, and the term was later extended to include the entire sector to the south.

The *K'inalha'* glyph is found in three other inscriptions at Dos Pilas. Stela 8 contains the most complete version, with both the **K'IN-NAL** sign and an "imix monster," probably a head variant for **HA** (Fig. 103a). *K'inalha'* appears after two verbs (*tun*-over-hand and "scattering") and directly before the name of Ruler 2. Evidently, this passage refers to rites at 9.14.0.0.0, recorded at the beginning of the passage. But this is not the dedicatory date of Stela 8. Rather, it is the date of Stela 15, at El Duende, suggesting that the phrase on Stela 8 commemorates rites that specifically took place at *K'inalha'*, or El Duende. The place name also occurs on Stela 1, just after a "scattering" verb (Fig. 103b). Although Stela 1 (9.13.15.0.0) is located in the main plaza of Dos Pilas, the text may record an event that occurred at El Duende. Stela 1 bears the earliest known reference to *K'inalha'*, so the tradition of erecting monuments at El Duende may not yet have begun.[17] The final record occurs on the recently discovered Panel 19, which appears to show that Ruler 3 of Dos Pilas "witnessed" events at both El Duende and the Plaza; alternatively, the "Plaza" glyph may simply be the more generalized reference to Dos Pilas, with the preceding glyph specifying a location within the site.

Names for buildings or building complexes have also been detected in separate work by Stuart, who was among the first to investigate struc-

[17] However, this suggestion cannot be demonstrated, because there are at least three eroded stelae near El Duende.

ture names in Maya script. His methods, however, differed from those here. He concentrated on a set of verbs that describes events (possibly dedication rites involving censing) in or involving "houses" (otot). These expressions conform to a formula, often invoking the names of temples with the phrase u-k'aba y-otot, "the name of the house of. . . ." Figure 104 presents a list of possible building names identified to date. Many of the "temple" names take the suffix -na(h), another term for "house," a pattern especially common at Palenque.

In summary, Maya inscriptions contain specific references to the location of rites within sites. Several expressions, including the ut-i phrase and the verb-location grouping, provide clues as to the location and name of such places. A number of toponyms refer to large sectors of a site—the El Duende glyph is one such place sign, in which the name for a single geographical feature has been applied to a more extensive area, including not only the eponymous spring but the surrounding hills and ravines as well. Other place signs refer to single structures or temples. But what is perhaps most striking is that, as with "foliage stones/stelae," the idiom for referring to human constructions is often a metaphor for "hill." The geography of the Classic Maya apparently involved a conceit in which there existed substantial overlap between natural and artificial categories.

a

u ti    ye ma la    K'UK' LAKAM    wi tsi    LAKAM HA'

b

Fig. 99 Place name from the Cross Group, Palenque

(a) Temple 18, Doorjamb: D17–D19 (drawing by David Stuart)

(b) Temple 18 (Schele and Mathews 1979: nos. 413, 472, 494).

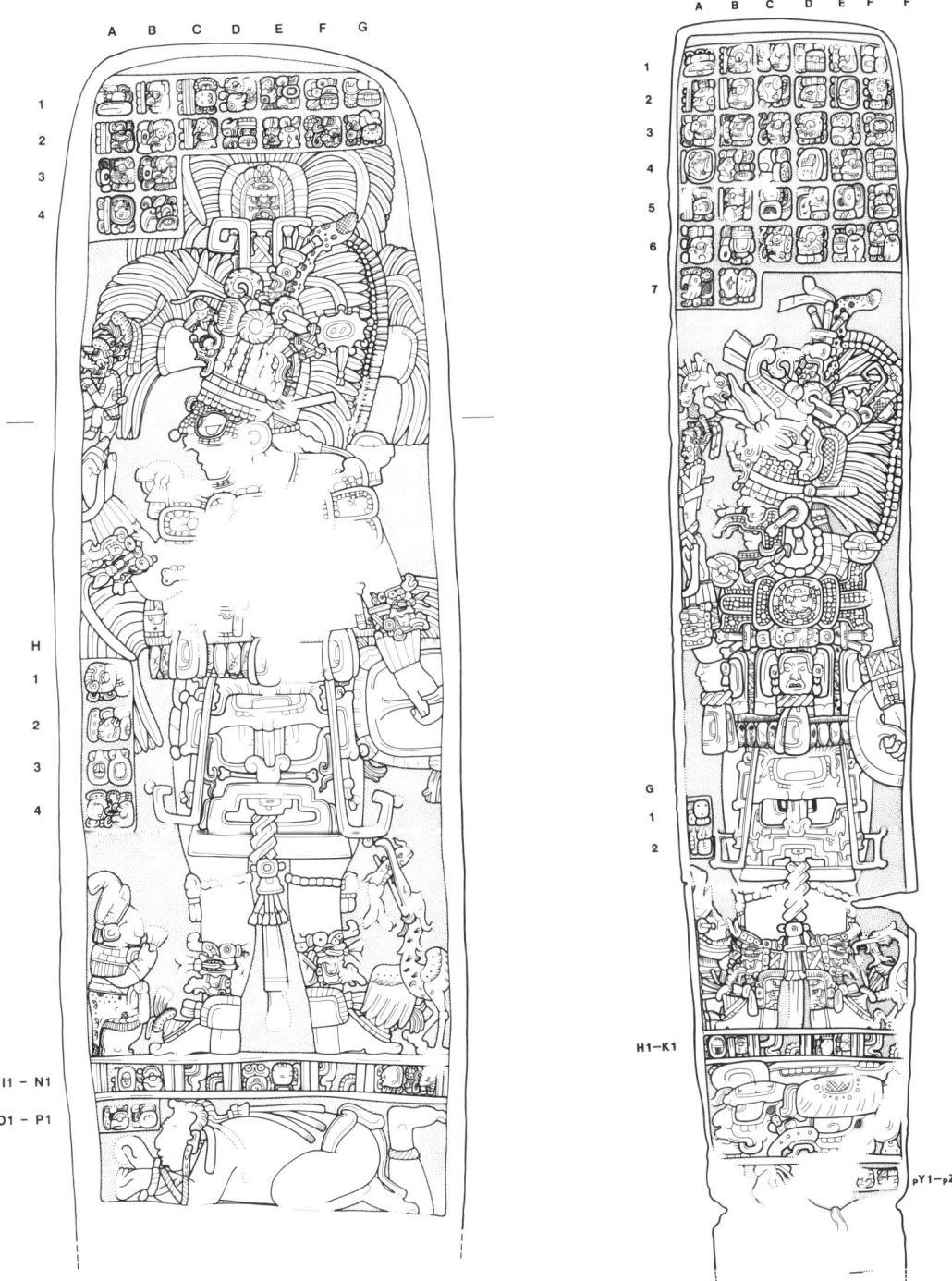

Fig. 100 Dos Pilas Stela 14 (drawing by Stephen Houston).

Fig. 101 Dos Pilas Stela 15 (drawing by Stephen Houston).

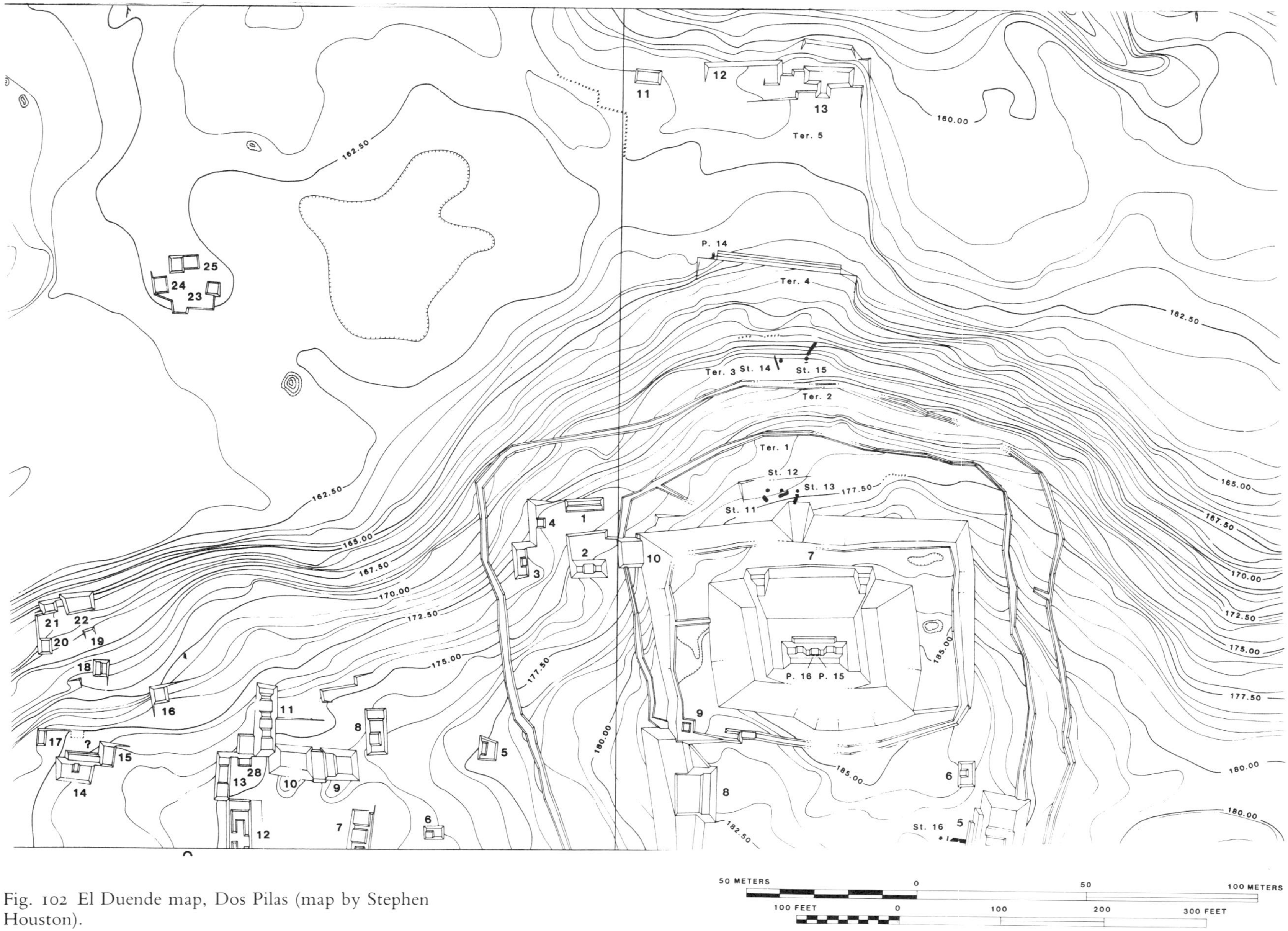

Fig. 102 El Duende map, Dos Pilas (map by Stephen Houston).

**a**      **b**      **c**

Fig. 103 Place names from Dos Pilas

(a) Stela 8: H6–I6 (unpublished drawing by Ian
    Graham)
(b) Stela 1: A5 (drawing from original)

(c) Stela 15: F3 (drawing by David Stuart).

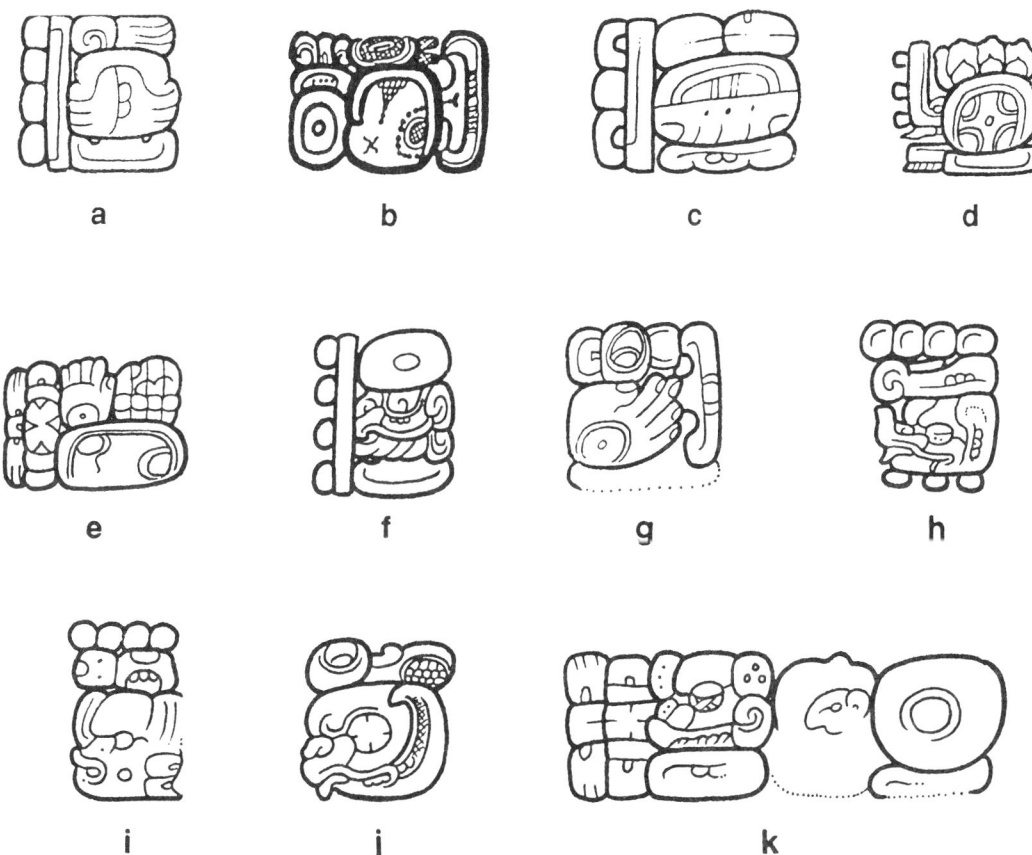

**a**      **b**      **c**      **d**

**e**      **f**      **g**      **h**

**i**      **j**      **k**

Fig. 104 A selection of building names

(a) Palenque Temple of the Inscriptions, F Panel: T11
    (after drawing by Linda Schele)
(b) Palenque Tablet of the 96 Glyphs: F6 (drawing
    by Linda Schele)
(c) Palenque Temple of the Cross, East Jamb: A1
    (drawing by David Stuart)
(d) Palenque Temple of the Foliated Cross, Alfarda:
    H1 (after drawing by Linda Schele in Lounsbury
    1980: fig. 5)
(e) Palenque Temple of the Foliated Cross, Doorjamb:
    B7 (after drawing by Linda Schele)

(f) Palenque Temple of the Sun, Alfarda: H1 (after
    drawing by Linda Schele in Lounsbury 1980:
    fig. 7)
(g) Palenque Palace Tablet: Q14 (after drawing by
    Linda Schele)
(h) Yaxchilan Hieroglyphic Stairway 3: B1b (after
    *CMHI* 3: 170)
(i) Yaxchilan Lintel 23: M6 (after *CMHI* 3: 136)
(j) Yaxchilan Lintel 21: B7 (after *CMHI* 3: 49)
(k) Yaxchilan Lintel 31: I5, J5 (after *CMHI* 3: 71).

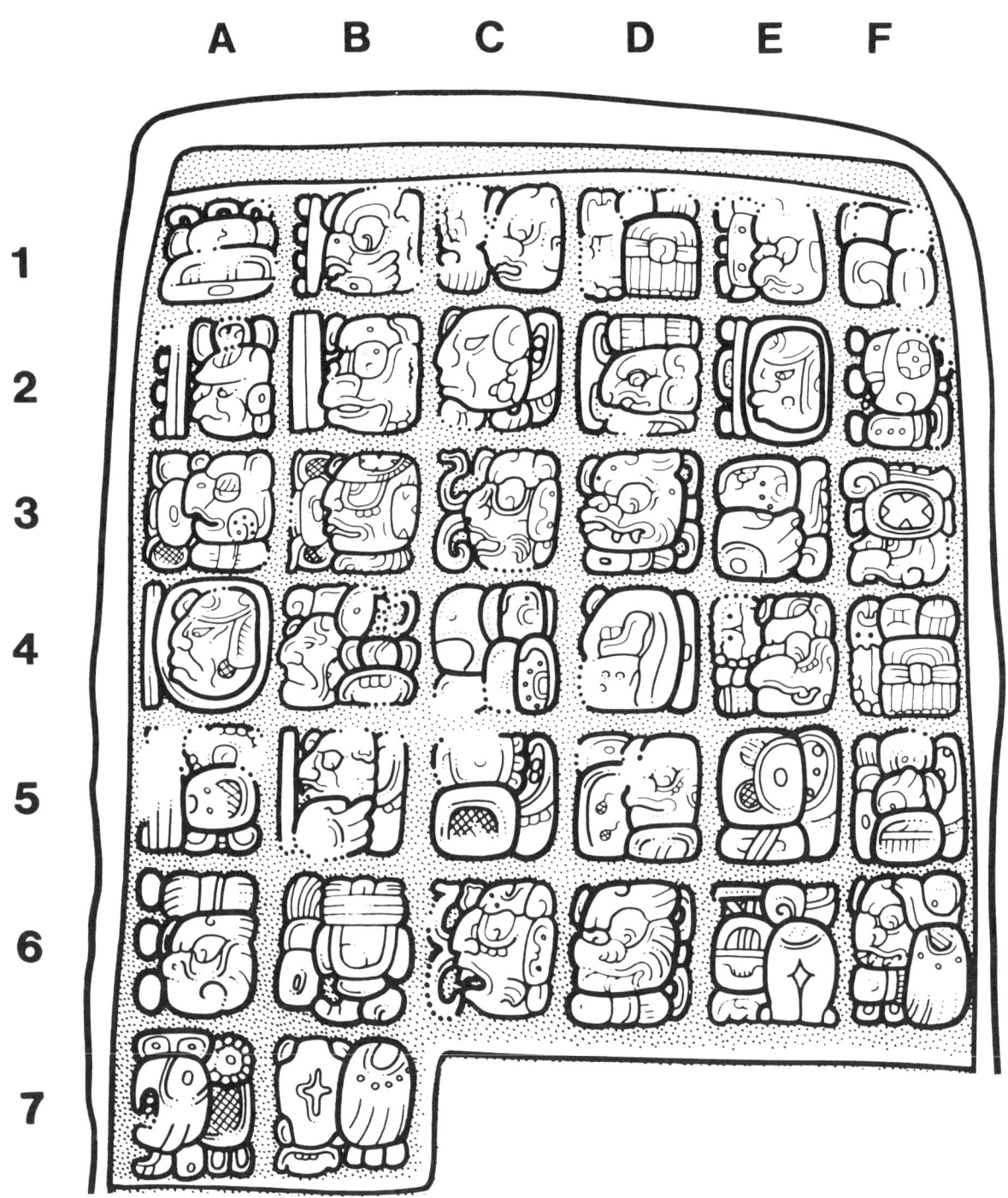

A B C D E F

1
2
3
4
5
6
7

Fig. 105 Upper text on Dos Pilas Stela 15 (drawing by Stephen Houston).

CHAPTER 7

# Place Names in Maya Texts: Two Case Studies

Preceding sections of this study have been concerned with the identification of specific place glyphs in Maya inscriptions. But the recognition of place names is only the first step toward understanding their broader significance in Maya texts. In this section we show how the identification of place names helps elucidate not only the readings of certain inscriptions, but the ritual and political events recorded by the Maya.

Our first case study is Stela 15 from El Duende, Dos Pilas (Fig. 105). Stela 15 is chiefly distinguished by the pristine condition of its carving and by its basal glyph, read *K'inalha'*, probably referring to the main architectural complex at El Duende. Moreover, the inscription above the portrait of Ruler 2 is unusual in that it contains five distinct place names, each in association with a different event.

The inscription opens with a Long Count date of 9.14.10.0.0, falling on the Calendar Round 5 Ahau 3 Mac. The initial verb at A7 reads, roughly, "he cast drops," and the location is specified immediately after, at B7. The subject of the event is Ruler 2, the "Divine Lord of Dos Pilas." Like the place names of Dos Pilas and El Duende, the place sign at B7 is based on the logograph **HA.** Its distin-

guishing quatrefoil element resembles a toponym mentioned both at Machaquila and on Stela 8 from Seibal (see Fig. 37). As an iconographic element, the quatrefoil image is even more widespread, appearing, for example, at Copan, where it supports the feet of Ruler 16 ("Yax Pac") on the sculpted jambs of Temple 18. Whether the glyph signifies a specific location is unclear, especially in light of its broad distribution.[18]

The second passage of the inscription (Blocks C1–D4) begins with the verb *naw-ah*, "was adorned" (Bricker 1986: 195). The subject is something owned or possessed by "Smoke G1," a nickname for a locally important deity. The next sentence consists of *ut-i* and the place glyph for Seibal, probably specifying where the object was adorned. Next comes a passage describing the erection of a *lakamtun*, or "large stone" (the ancient term for "stela") of "Smoke G1," followed by *ut-i* (at D6) and the cleft hill place name of Aguateca (E1). Presumably, a stela (yet to be found) was dedicated at Aguateca on the same day as the Seibal "adornment" ceremony and Ruler 2's casting of drops, possibly of blood (Stuart 1988a).

The closing section of the inscription (E2–F4)

[18] According to Nikolai Grube and Linda Schele, the sign refers generally to "plazas," an identification based on its occurrence at Machaquila (see above). The idea is an interest- ing one, but it cannot be proven without a precise phonetic decipherment.

tells us that eighty days after these events, on 7 Ahau 3 Kayab, Ruler 2 dedicated a stone at El Duende. The stone is surely Stela 15 itself. Finally, the text ends (at E5–F6) by mentioning a ritual dance (Nikolai Grube, personal communication, 1990), followed by *ut-i* and the Dos Pilas place glyph (F6), noting where the dance took place. Taken as a whole, Stela 15 with its five place glyphs clearly illustrates the importance of location in the record of dedicatory rituals. Each event is explicitly linked with a toponym, even if the personal name of the actor or protagonist is omitted.

Our second brief case study is Hieroglyphic Stairway 1 of Seibal (Fig. 106). According to dates and toponyms on the monument, it appears that Ruler 4 of Dos Pilas scattered at two different locations—once at Seibal, and then two days later at Tamarindito. The distance between Seibal and Tamarindito is such that Ruler 4 was probably moving at a fast pace, since the sites are located a days' hike from one another. The inscription has two other implications, one being that Classic rulers described circuits, performing rituals at subordinate sites (Houston and Stuart n.d.), the other that Ruler 4 exercised sway over a site that was soon to wage war on him (Houston and Mathews 1985).

By tracing the movements of people and events in this way, we see at Dos Pilas and Seibal how place glyphs can add a previously unknown physical dimension to narrative records, whether ritual or historical in nature. Yet it is always important to remember that these inscriptions are "court reports" that chronicle the *official* movements and actions of Maya rulers, regardless of whether they were in fact present. In any event, we realize that the study of such place references in Maya inscriptions is only beginning, and are hopeful that such information will be of use to the epigrapher and archaeologist alike.

Fig. 106 Texts from Seibal Hieroglyphic Stairway 1

(a) P2b–R2, V2a–W1, at an event taking place at 9.15.14.17.18 (after unpublished drawing by Ian Graham)

(b) X1a–W2, Y1–Z2, at an event taking place at 9.15.15.0.0 (after unpublished drawing by Ian Graham).

# Conclusions

Place names were central to the symbol systems of ancient Mesoamerica. Indeed, the hieroglyphic writing of Central Mexican cultures dealt with very little else. In this paper we have presented evidence that such place glyphs are equally common in Maya script, and not in the form of Emblem Glyphs, as some epigraphers have supposed. Figure 107 presents a map showing the Classic sites as the ancient Maya themselves would have labeled them.

The proposed place glyphs consistently follow an expression signifying "it happened," as well as a possible locative statement meaning "within." The locative appears to be optional, much like locatives in the "shell-star" war event. In addition, we have developed and defended the proposition that these compounds vary by site rather than by polity, and that they constitute true toponyms, or place names. A probable paraphrase of the expression is, "it happened within X," with X being a specific location. Some examples suggest X as a specific place within a site. The event to which the expression refers appears before, in a separate and larger sentence.

The relation between Emblem Glyphs and toponyms remains indistinct. Some, but perhaps not all Emblem Glyph main signs probably originated as place names. The best examples of this come from Tikal and Yaxha, where the main signs of the local Emblems consistently appear after *ut-i*. But in those cases where the main sign is distinct from the true place name, as at Dos Pilas, Aguateca, and Palenque, it is perhaps because the places formed part of larger polities made up of more than one large center. In historical perspective, specific place names might have enjoyed greater use than Emblem Glyphs during the first part of the Early Classic period, as appears to have been true at Tikal. The simultaneous use of toponym and Emblem Glyph in a single clause is a relatively late innovation that perhaps reflects the growth of polities to a point where they incorporated additional major centers (Houston 1993).

The presence of "true" place names in the inscriptions relates also to the question of how sites were identified and subdivided within by the Classic Maya. Evidence from Dos Pilas and Palenque provides faint suggestions of internal subdivision, yet the contexts in which these references appear seem ambiguous at the present time. At the very least, Classic Period scribes probably recorded the names of sites in addition to identifying individual structures and the persons who commissioned them.

In a number of instances we have identified toponyms that are phonetically transparent, but semantically obscure. Examples include those from Naranjo (**ma-xa-ma**) and Copan (**OX-wi-ti-ki**). We suspect that, as with many place names, these words are of great antiquity, with origins deep in the Preclassic era. Possibly even the Late Classic Maya did not understand them.

The proposals in this report are not conclusive

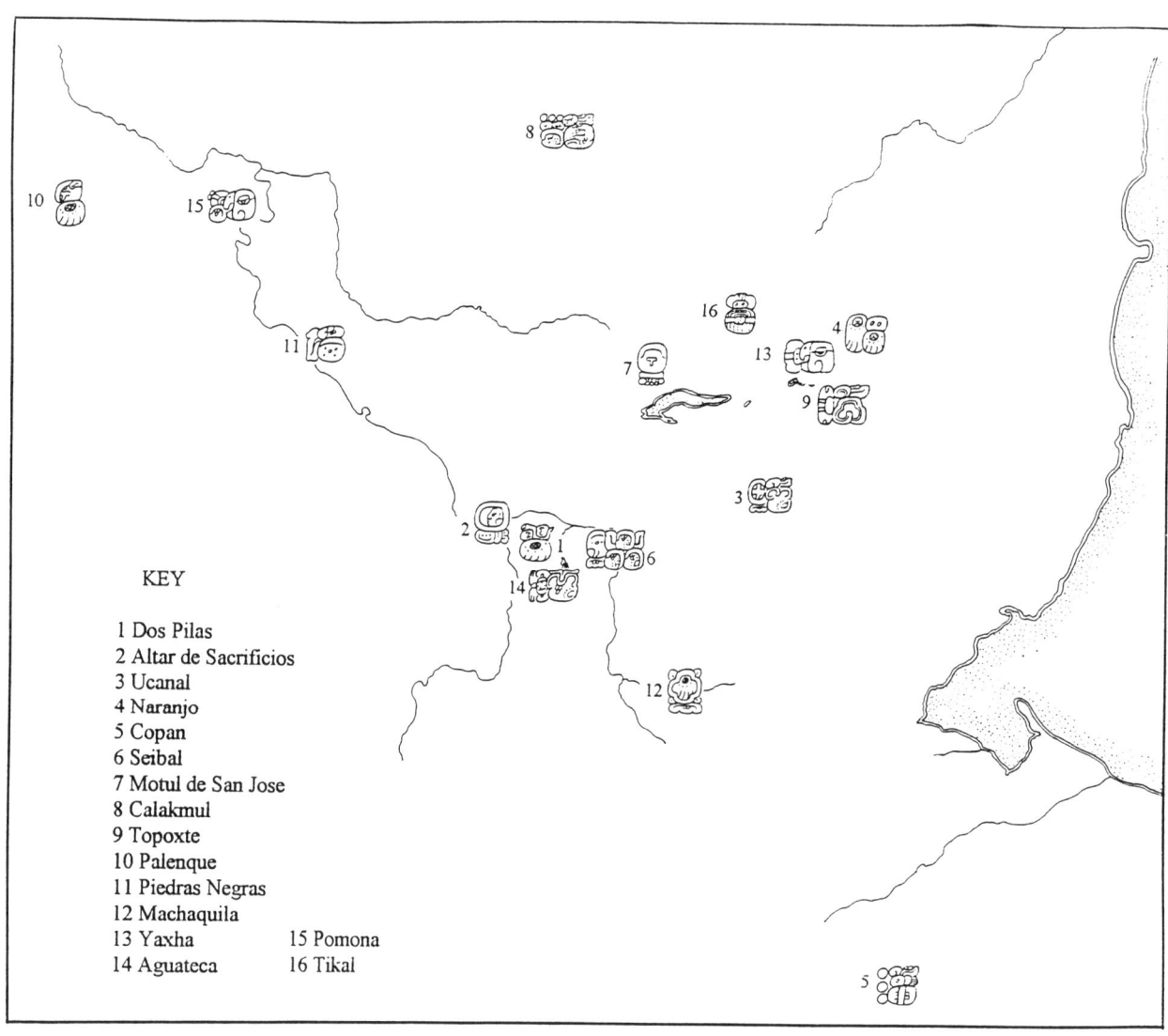

Fig. 107 Classic Maya Place Names

KEY

1 Dos Pilas
2 Altar de Sacrificios
3 Ucanal
4 Naranjo
5 Copan
6 Seibal
7 Motul de San Jose
8 Calakmul
9 Topoxte
10 Palenque
11 Piedras Negras
12 Machaquila
13 Yaxha          15 Pomona
14 Aguateca       16 Tikal

findings. Rather, they are offered as suggestions warranting further discussion by Mayanists. Many details of syntax and meaning in the texts described here still need to be clarified, as do a number of possible place glyphs omitted from consideration. Yet the evidence for the existence of Classic Maya place names seems strong, to say nothing of the important need they would seem to fill in the Maya inscriptional record. The priority of future work must be to decipher the remaining place references so as to determine their nature once and for all, and to interpret more precisely the hieroglyphic compounds that accompany them.

In closing, we would like to emphasize that these preliminary data on Maya place glyphs have the potential to address questions that go far beyond mere epigraphic concerns. Decipherments seldom are important for their own sake but are significant for what they might someday tell us about ancient Maya society, politics, religion, and history. In the case of place names we gain insights into how the Maya named and structured landscapes. What remains for the future is an integration of such emic geographical concepts with the etic patterns documented by settlement pattern archaeology.

# Bibliography

AYALA FALCÓN, MARICELA
  1987  La estela 39 de Tikal, Mundo Perdido. *Memorias del Primer Coloquio Internacional de Mayistas, 5–10 de Agosto de 1985:* 599–654. Universidad Nacional Autónoma de México, México.

BARRERA VÁSQUEZ, ALFREDO (COMPILER)
  1980  *Diccionario Maya Cordemex: Maya-Español, Español-Maya.* Ediciones Cordemex, Mérida, Yucatan.

BARTHEL, THOMAS S.
  1952  Der Morgensternkult in den Darstellungen der Dresdener Mayahandschrift. *Ethnos* 17: 73–112.
  1953  Regionen des Regengottes. *Ethnos* 18: 86–105.
  1968  El complejo "emblema." *Estudios de Cultura Maya* 7: 159–193.

BECQUELIN, PIERRE, and CLAUDE F. BAUDEZ
  1982  *Tonina, une cité Maya du Chiapas.* Mission arquèologique et ethnologique Français au Mexique, collection études Mésoaméricains 6 (3). Editions Recherche sur les Civilisations, Paris.

BEETZ, CARL P., and LINTON SATTERTHWAITE
  1981  *The Monuments and Inscriptions of Caracol, Belize.* University Museum Monograph 45. The University Museum, University of Pennsylvania, Philadelphia.

BERJONNEAU, GÉRALD, and JEAN-LOUIS SONNERY (EDS.)
  1985  *Rediscovered Masterpieces of Mesoamerica: Mexico–Guatemala–Honduras.* Editions Arts 135, Boulogne.

BERLIN, B., D. E. BREEDLOVE, and P. H. RAVEN
  1974  *Principles of Tzeltal Plant Classification.* Academic Press, New York.

BERLIN, HEINRICH
  1958  El glifo "emblema" en las inscripciones Mayas. *Journal de la Société des Américanistes* 47: 111–119.
  1963  The Palenque Triad. *Journal de la Société des Américanistes* 52: 91–99.

  1968  *The Tablet of the 96 Glyphs at Palenque, Chiapas, Mexico.* Middle American Research Institute, Pub. 26: 135–150. Tulane University, New Orleans.

BEYER, HERMANN
  1937  *Studies on the Inscriptions of Chichen Itza.* Carnegie Institution of Washington, Pub. 483. Washington, D.C.

BRICKER, VICTORIA R.
  1986  *A Grammar of Mayan Hieroglyphs.* Middle American Research Institute, Pub. 56. Tulane University, New Orleans.

BRODA, JOHANNA
  1987  The Provenience of the Offering: Tribute and *Cosmovisión.* In *The Aztec Templo Mayor* (Elizabeth Hill Boone, ed.): 211–256. Dumbarton Oaks, Washington, D.C.

CAMPBELL, LYLE
  n.d.  There is No "Highland" Input in Mayan Hieroglyphic Writing! Unpublished ms., 1989.

CASO, ALFONSO
  1928  *Las estelas zapotecas.* Secretaría de Educación Pública, México.
  1949  El mapa de Teozacoalco. *Cuadernos Americanos* 8 (5): 145–181.

CIVIL, MIGUEL
  1976  Lexicography. In *Sumerological Studies in Honor of Thorkild Jacobsen on His Seventieth Birthday, June 7, 1974* (Stephen J. Lieberman, ed.): 123–157. The Oriental Institute of the University of Chicago, Assyriological Studies, No. 20. University of Chicago Press, Chicago.

CIVIL, MIGUEL, and R. D. BIGGS
  1966  Notes sur des textes sumeriens archaiques. *Revue d'Assyriologie* 60: 1–16.

CLOSS, MICHAEL P.
  1988  A Phonetic Version of the Maya Glyph for North. *American Antiquity* 53 (2): 386–393.

CMHI, or *Corpus of Maya Hieroglyphic Inscriptions*
  See  Graham 1978, 1979, 1980, 1982; Graham and Von Euw 1975, 1977.

COE, MICHAEL D.
   1973   *The Maya Scribe and His World.* The Grolier
          Club, New York.
COE, MICHAEL D., AND ELIZABETH P. BENSON
   1966   Three Maya Relief Panels at Dumbarton
          Oaks. *Studies in Pre-Columbian Art and Archae-
          ology* 2. Dumbarton Oaks, Washington, D.C.
COE, WILLIAM R.
   1967   *Tikal: A Handbook of the Ancient Maya Ruins.*
          The University Museum, University of Penn-
          sylvania, Philadelphia.
CULBERT, T. PATRICK (ED.)
   1991   *Classic Maya Political History: Hieroglyphic and
          Archaeological Evidence.* Cambridge University
          Press, Cambridge.
DE VOS, JAN
   1980   *La Paz de Dios y del Rey: La Conquista de la
          Selva Lacandona, 1525–1821.* Fonapas Chiapas,
          Mexico.
DIAKONOFF, I. M.
   1976   Ancient Writing and Ancient Written Lan-
          guage: Pitfalls and Peculiarities in the Study of
          Sumerian. In *Sumerological Studies in Honor of
          Thorkild Jacobsen on His Seventieth Birthday,
          June 7, 1974* (Stephen J. Lieberman, ed.): 99–
          121. The Oriental Institute of the University
          of Chicago, Assyriological Studies, No. 20.
          University of Chicago Press, Chicago.
FASH, BARBARA, WILLIAM FASH, SHEREE LANE, RUDY
LARIOS, LINDA SCHELE, JEFF STOMPER, and DAVID
STUART
   1992   Investigations of a Classic Maya Council
          House at Copán, Honduras. *Journal of Field
          Archaeology* 19(4): 419–442.
FOX, JAMES A., and JOHN S. JUSTESON
   1984   Polyvalence in Mayan Hieroglyphic Writing.
          In *Phoneticism in Mayan Hieroglyphic Writing*
          (John S. Justeson and Lyle Campbell, eds.):
          17–76. Institute for Mesoamerican Studies,
          State University of New York at Albany,
          Pub. 9. Albany.
GANN, THOMAS
   1900   Mounds in Northern Honduras. *Bureau of
          American Ethnology 19th Annual Report, Pt. 2:*
          655–692. Smithsonian Institution, Washing-
          ton, D.C.
GRAHAM, IAN
   1967   *Archaeological Explorations in El Peten, Guate-
          mala.* Middle American Research Institute,
          Pub. 33. Tulane University, New Orleans.
   1978   *Naranjo, Chunhuitz, Xunantunich. Corpus of
          Maya Hieroglyphic Inscriptions* 2 (2). Peabody
          Museum of Archaeology and Ethnology, Har-
          vard University, Cambridge.
   1979   *Yaxchilan. Corpus of Maya Hieroglyphic In-
          scriptions* 3 (2). Peabody Museum of Archaeol-
          ogy and Ethnology, Harvard University,
          Cambridge.
   1980   *Ixkun, Ucanal, Ixtutz, Naranjo. Corpus of Maya
          Hieroglyphic Inscriptions* 2 (3). Peabody Mu-
          seum of Archaeology and Ethnology, Har-
          vard University, Cambridge.
   1982   *Yaxchilan. Corpus of Maya Hieroglyphic In-
          scriptions* 3 (3). Peabody Museum of Archae-
          ology and Ethnology, Harvard University,
          Cambridge.
   1988   Homeless Hieroglyphs. *Antiquity* 62: 122–
          125.
GRAHAM, IAN, and ERIC VON EUW
   1975   *Naranjo. Corpus of Maya Hieroglyphic Inscriptions*
          2 (1). Peabody Museum of Archaeology and
          Ethnology, Harvard University, Cambridge.
   1977   *Yaxchilan. Corpus of Maya Hieroglyphic In-
          scriptions* 3 (1). Peabody Museum of Archae-
          ology and Ethnology, Harvard University,
          Cambridge.
GRAHAM, JOHN
   1972   *The Hieroglyphic Inscriptions and Monumental
          Art of Altar de Sacrificios.* Papers of the Pea-
          body Museum of Archaeology and Ethnol-
          ogy, Harvard University, 64 (2). Cambridge.
GRUBE, NIKOLAI, and WERNER NAHM
   1990   *A Sign for the Syllable* **mi.** Research Reports
          on Ancient Maya Writing 33. Center for
          Maya Research, Washington, D.C.
GUITERAS-HOLMES, CALIXTA
   1961   *Perils of the Soul: The World View of a Tzotzil
          Indian.* Free Press, Glencoe, New York.
HALL, GRANT D., STANLEY M. TARKA JR., W. JEFFREY
HURST, DAVID STUART, and RICHARD E.W. ADAMS
   1990   Cacao Residues in Ancient Maya Vessels from
          Rio Azul, Guatemala. *American Antiquity* 55
          (1): 138–143.
HOPKINS, NICHOLAS A.
   1991   Classic and Modern Relationship Terms and
          the "Child of Mother" Glyph (TI: 606.23). In
          *Sixth Palenque Round Table, 1986* (Virginia M.
          Fields and Merle Green Robertson, eds.):
          255–265. University of Oklahoma Press,
          Norman.
HOUSTON, STEPHEN D.
   1984   An Example of Homophony in Maya Script.
          *American Antiquity* 49: 790–805.
   1986   Problematic Emblem Glyphs: Examples from
          Altar de Sacrificios, El Chorro, Rio Azul, and
          Xultun. *Research Reports on Ancient Maya Writ-
          ing* 3. Center for Maya Research, Washing-
          ton, D.C.
   1989   Archaeology and Maya Writing. *Journal of
          World Prehistory* 3 (1): 1–32.
   1993   *History and Hieroglyphs at Dos Pilas: Dynastic
          Politics of the Classic Maya.* University of
          Texas Press, Austin.
HOUSTON, STEPHEN D., and PETER MATHEWS
   1985   *The Dynastic Sequence of Dos Pilas, Guatemala.*
          Pre-Columbian Art Research Institute, Mono-
          graph 1. San Francisco.
HOUSTON, STEPHEN D., and DAVID STUART
   n.d.   Placenames and Rituals of the Late Classic
          Maya. Unpublished ms., 1989.

HOUSTON, STEPHEN, DAVID STUART, and KARL TAUBE

1989    Folk Classification of Classic Maya Pottery. *American Anthropologist* 9: 720–726.

1992    Image and Text on the "Jauncy Vase." In *The Maya Vase Book: A Corpus of Rollout Photographs of Maya Vases* 3 (Justin Kerr, ed.): 498–512. Kerr Associates, New York.

JONES, CHRISTOPHER, and LINTON SATTERTHWAITE

1982    *The Monuments and Inscriptions at Tikal: The Carved Monuments.* Tikal Report 33 (A). The University Museum, University of Pennsylvania, Philadelphia.

JOSSERAND, J. KATHRYN, and NICHOLAS A. HOPKINS

n.d.    Final Performance Report: National Endowment for the Humanities Grant, RT-20643-86, Chol (Mayan) Dictionary Database, 1988.

JUSTESON, JOHN S.

1975    The Identification of the Emblem Glyph of Yaxha, El Peten. *Contributions of the University of California Archaeological Research Facility* 27: 123–129.

1984    Interpretations of Mayan Hieroglyphs. Appendix B in *Phoneticism in Mayan Hieroglyphic Writing* (John S. Justeson and Lyle Campbell, eds.): 315–362. Institute for Mesoamerican Studies, State University of New York at Albany, Pub. 9. Albany.

JUSTESON, JOHN S., and PETER MATHEWS

1983    The Seating of the *Tun:* Further Evidence concerning a Late Preclassic Lowlands Maya Stela Cult. *American Antiquity* 48: 586–593.

KAUFMAN, TERRENCE S., and WILLIAM M. NORMAN

1984    An Outline of Proto-Cholan Phonology, Morphology, and Vocabulary. In *Phoneticism in Mayan Hieroglyphic Writing* (Lyle Campbell and John S. Justeson, eds.): 77–167. Institute for Mesoamerican Studies, State University of New York at Albany, Pub. 9. Albany.

KELLEY, DAVID H.

1976    *Deciphering the Maya Script.* University of Texas Press, Austin.

KERR, JUSTIN

1989    *The Maya Vase Book: A Corpus of Rollout Photographs of Maya Vases* 1. Kerr Associates, New York.

1990    *The Maya Vase Book: A Corpus of Rollout Photographs of Maya Vases* 2. Kerr Associates, New York.

KNOROSOV, YURII V.

1967    Selected Chapters from the Writing of the Maya Indians (Sophie Coe, trans.). *Russian Translation Series,* No. 4. Peabody Museum of Archaeology and Ethnology, Harvard University, Cambridge.

KOWALSKI, JEFF K.

1986    Uxmal: A Terminal Classic Maya Capital in Northern Yucatan. In *City-States of the Maya: Art and Architecture* (Elizabeth P. Benson, ed.): 138–171. Rocky Mountain Institute for Pre-Columbian Studies, Denver.

KROCHOK, RUTH

1989    Hieroglyphic Inscriptions at Chichén Itzá, Yucatán, México: The Temples of the Initial Series, the One Lintel, the Three Lintels, and the Four Lintels. *Research Reports on Ancient Maya Writing* 23. Center for Maya Research, Washington, D.C.

LAMB, DANA, and GINGER LAMB

1951    *Quest for the Lost City.* Harper, New York.

LIZARDI RAMOS, CÉSAR

1961    Las Estelas 4 y 5 de Balancan-Morales, Tabasco. *Estudios de Cultura Maya* 1: 107–130.

1963    Inscripciones de Pomoná, Tabasco, México. *Estudios de Cultura Maya* 3: 187–202.

LOUNSBURY, FLOYD G.

1973    On the Derivation and Reading of the "Ben-Ich" Prefix. In *Mesoamerican Writing Systems* (Elizabeth P. Benson, ed.): 99–143. Dumbarton Oaks, Washington, D.C.

1974    Descriptive Note for Cover Illustration. In *Primera Mesa Redonda de Palenque (1)* (Merle Greene Robertson, ed.). The Robert Louis Stevenson School, Pebble Beach, California.

1980    Some Problems in the Interpretation of the Mythological Portion of the Hieroglyphic Text of the Temple of the Cross at Palenque. In *Third Palenque Round Table, 1978 (2)* (Merle Green Robertson, ed.): 99–115. University of Texas Press, Austin.

MACLEOD, BARBARA

1990    The God N/Step Set in the Primary Standard Sequence. In *The Maya Vase Book: A Corpus of Rollout Photographs of Maya Vases* 2 (Justin Kerr, ed.): 331–347. Kerr Associates, New York.

MALER, TEOBERT

1903    Researches in the Central Portion of the Usumatsintla Valley; Reports of Explorations for the Museum, Part Second. *Memoirs of the Peabody Museum of American Archaeology and Ethnology, Harvard University* 2 (2). Cambridge.

1908a   Explorations in the Department of Peten, Guatemala, and Adjacent Region: Topoxte; Yaxhá; Benque Viejo; Naranjo. *Memoirs of the Peabody Museum of American Archaeology and Ethnology, Harvard University* 4 (2). Cambridge.

1908b   Explorations of the Upper Usumatsintla and Adjacent Region: Altar de Sacrificios; Seibal; Itsimté-Sácluk; Cankuen. *Memoirs of the Peabody Museum of American Archaeology and Ethnology, Harvard University* 4 (1). Cambridge.

1910    Explorations in the Department of Peten, Guatemala and Adjacent Region: Motul de San José; Peten-Itza, Reports of Explorations for the Museum. *Memoirs of the Peabody Museum of American Archaeology and Ethnology, Harvard University* 4 (3). Cambridge.

MARCUS, JOYCE

1976    *Emblem and State in the Classic Maya Lowlands: An Epigraphic Approach to Territorial Organization.* Dumbarton Oaks, Washington, D.C.

MARHENKE, RANDA
  1989  A Note on the "ADI-Title" Glyph. In *U Mut Maya II* (Tom Jones and Carolyn Young, eds.): 59–61. U MUT MAYA, Arcata.
MATHEWS, PETER
  1979  The Glyphs on the Ear Ornaments from Tomb A-1/1. In *Excavations at Altun Ha, Belize, 1964–1970* (David Pendergast, ed.): 79–80. Royal Ontario Museum, Toronto.
  1985  Maya Early Classic Monuments and Inscriptions. In *A Consideration of the Early Classic Period in the Maya Lowlands* (Gordon R. Willey and Peter Mathews, eds.): 5–54. Institute for Mesoamerican Studies, State University of New York at Albany, Pub. 10. Albany.
  1991  Classic Maya Emblem Glyphs. In *Classic Maya Political History: Hieroglyphic and Archaeological Evidence* (T. Patrick Culbert, ed.): 19–29. A School of American Research Book. Cambridge University Press, Cambridge.
  n.d.a  On the Glyphs "West" and "Mah K'ina." Unpublished ms., 1979.
  n.d.b  The Emblem Glyphs of Ucanal, Sacul, and Ixtutz. Unpublished ms., 1977.
  n.d.c  The Inscription on the Back of Stela 8, Dos Pilas, Guatemala. Unpublished ms., 1979.
  n.d.d  Notes on "Site Q." Unpublished ms., 1979.
  n.d.e  Emblem Glyphs in Classic Maya Inscriptions. Paper presented at the 83rd Meeting of the American Anthropological Association, Denver, Colorado, 1984.
MATHEWS, PETER, and JOHN S. JUSTESON
  1984  Patterns of Sign Substitution in Maya Hieroglyphic Writing: The "Affix Cluster." In *Phoneticism in Mayan Hieroglyphic Writing* (John S. Justeson and Lyle Campbell, eds.): 185–232. Institute for Mesoamerican Studies, State University of New York at Albany, Pub. 9. Albany.
MAUDSLAY, ALFRED P.
  1889–  *Archaeology: Biologia Centrali-Americana* 1 (text,
  1902   plates). R. H. Porter and Dulau, London.
MAYER, KARL HERBERT
  1989  *Maya Monuments: Sculptures of Unknown Provenance, Suppl. 2.* Verlag von Flemming, Berlin.
MICHALOWSKI, PIOTR
  1991  Early Mesopotamian Communicative Systems: Art, Literature, and Writing. In *Investigating Artistic Environments in the Ancient Near East* (Ann C. Gunter, ed.): 53–69. Arthur M. Sackler Gallery, Smithsonian Institution, Washington, D.C.
MILLER, JEFFREY H.
  1974  Notes on a Stelae Pair Probably from Calakmul, Campeche, Mexico. In *First Palenque Round Table, 1973: Part 1* (Merle Green Robertson, ed.): 149–161. The Robert Louis Stevenson School, Pebble Beach, California.
MILLER, MARY E., and STEPHEN D. HOUSTON
  1987  The Classic Maya Ballgame and Its Architectural Setting: A Study in Relations Between Text and Image. *RES* 14: 47–66.

MONAGHAN, JOHN
  1990  Peformance and the Structure of the Mixtec Codices. *Ancient Mesoamerica* 1 (1): 133–140.
MORLEY, SYLVANUS G.
  1937  *The Inscriptions of the Peten.* Carnegie Institu-
  –38   tion of Washington, Pub. 437. Washington, D.C.
NAVARRETE, CARLOS, and LUIS LUJÁN MUÑOZ
  1963  Reconocimiento arqueológico del sitio de "Dos Pilas," Petexbatún, Guatemala. *Cuadernos de Antropología* 2. Instituto de Investigaciones Históricas, Universidad de San Carlos de Guatemala, Guatemala.
NORMAN, V. G.
  1973  *Izapa Sculpture.* New World Archaeological Foundation, Paper 30. Brigham Young University, Provo.
PEÑAFIEL, ANTONIO
  1885  *Nombres geográficos de México.* Secretaría de Fomento, México.
POHL, JOHN M.D., and BRUCE E. BYLAND
  1990  Mixtec Landscape Perception and Archaeological Settlement Patterns. *Ancient Mesoamerica* (1) 1: 113–131.
PORTER, JAMES B.
  1985  Relief Monuments. In *The Student's Guide to Archaeological Illustrating* (2nd rev. ed.) (Brian D. Dillon, ed.): 77–94. Archaeological Research Tools 1. Institute of Archaeology, University of California, Los Angeles.
PROSKOURIAKOFF, TATIANA
  1963  Historical Data in the Inscriptions of Yaxchilan, Part I. *Estudios de Cultura Maya* 3: 147–167.
  1973  The Hand-grasping-fish and Associated Glyphs on Classic Maya Monuments. In *Mesoamerican Writing Systems* (Elizabeth P. Benson, ed.): 165–178. Dumbarton Oaks, Washington, D.C.
  1974  Jades from the Cenote of Sacrifice, Chichen Itza, Yucatan, Mexico. *Memoirs of the Peabody Museum of Archaeology and Ethnology* 10 (1). Cambridge.
PULESTON, DENNIS
  1983  *The Settlement Survey of Tikal.* Tikal Report No. 13, University Museum Monograph 48 (William A. Haviland, ed.). The University Museum, University of Pennsylvania, Philadelphia.
RIESE, BERTHOLD
  1984  Kriegsberichte der klassischen Maya. *Baessler-Archiv, Beiträge zur Völkerkunde* 30 (2): 255–321.
RINGLE, WILLIAM M.
  1988  Of Mice and Monkeys: The Value and Meaning of T1016, the God C Hieroglyph. *Research Reports on Ancient Maya Writing* 18. Center for Maya Research, Washington, D.C.
ROBERTSON, MERLE GREENE
  1983  *The Sculpture of Palenque 1, The Temple of the Inscriptions.* Princeton University Press, Princeton.
  1985  *The Sculpture of Palenque: 3, The Late Buildings*

*of the Palace.* Princeton University Press, Princeton.

ROBICSEK, FRANCIS
1978   *The Smoking Gods: Tobacco in Maya Art, History, and Religion.* University of Oklahoma Press, Norman.

ROBICSEK, FRANCIS, and DONALD M. HALES
1981   *The Maya Book of the Dead: The Ceramic Codex, The Corpus of Codex Style Ceramics of the Late Classic Period.* University of Virginia Art Museum, Charlottesville, Virginia.

RUPPERT, KARL, and JOHN H. DENISON, JR.
1943   *Archaeological Reconnaissance in Campeche, Quintana Roo, and Peten.* Carnegie Institution of Washington, Pub. 543. Washington, D.C.

SÁENZ, CÉSAR A.
1956   *Exploraciones en la Pirámide de la Cruz Foliada.* Dirección de Monumentos Pre-hispánicos Informe 5. Instituto Nacional de Antropología e Historia, México.

SAPPER, KARL
1907   Choles und Chorties. *Congrès International des Américanistes, Quinzième Session, Québec, 10 au 15 Septembre, 1906* 2: 423–465. Karl W. Hiersemann, Leipzig.

SCHELE, LINDA
1982   *Maya Glyphs: The Verbs.* University of Texas Press, Austin.
1984a  Human Sacrifice among the Classic Maya. In *Ritual Human Sacrifice in Mesoamerica* (Elizabeth H. Boone, ed.): 6–48. Dumbarton Oaks, Washington, D.C.
1984b  Some Suggested Readings of the Event and Office of Heir-designate at Palenque. In *Phoneticism in Mayan Hieroglyphic Writing* (John S. Justeson and Lyle Campbell, eds.): 287–306. Institute for Mesoamerican Studies, State University of New York at Albany, Pub. 9. Albany.
1988   The Xibalba Shuffle: A Dance after Death. In *Maya Iconography* (Elizabeth P. Benson and Gillett G. Griffin, eds.): 294–317. Princeton University Press, Princeton.
n.d.   Post-Emblem Glyph and Directional Titles from Classic Maya Nominal Phrases. Paper presented at a Conference on Copan, University of California at Los Angeles, 1977.

SCHELE, LINDA, and DAVID FREIDEL
1990   *A Forest of Kings: The Untold Story of the Ancient Maya.* William Morrow, New York.

SCHELE, LINDA, and PETER MATHEWS
1979   *The Bodega of Palenque, Chiapas, Mexico.* Dumbarton Oaks, Washington, D.C.

SCHELE, LINDA, PETER MATHEWS, and FLOYD G. LOUNSBURY
n.d.   Parentage Expressions in Classic Maya Inscriptions. Paper presented at the International Conference on Maya Iconography and Hieroglyphic Writing, Guatemala City, 1977.

SCHELE, LINDA, and MARY ELLEN MILLER
1986   *The Blood of Kings: Dynasty and Ritual in Maya Art.* Kimbell Art Museum, Fort Worth.

SCHUMANN, OTTO
1973   *La lengua Chol de Tila (Chiapas).* Cuaderno 8. Centro de Estudios Mayas, Universidad Nacional Autónoma de México, México.

SLOCUM, MARIANNA, and FLORENCE L. GERDEL
1976   *Vocabulario Tzeltal de Bachajon.* Instituto Lingüístico de Verano, México.

STUART, DAVID
1978   Some Thoughts on Certain Occurrences of the T565 Glyph Element at Palenque. In *Tercera Mesa Redonda de Palenque 4* (Merle Greene Robertson and Donnan Call Jeffers, eds.): 167–171. Pre-Columbian Art Research Center, Palenque, Mexico.
1984   Royal Auto-Sacrifice among the Maya: A Study of Image and Meaning. *RES* 7/8: 6–20.
1985a  The "Count-of-Captives" Epithet in Classic Maya Writing. In *Fifth Palenque Round Table, 1983* (Virginia M. Fields and Merle Greene Robertson, eds.): 97–101. Pre-Columbian Art Research Institute, San Francisco.
1985b  The Yaxha Emblem Glyph as *Yax-ha. Research Reports on Ancient Maya Writing* 1. Center for Maya Research, Washington, D.C.
1987a  The Paintings of Tomb 12, Rio Azul. In *Rio Azul Reports 3, The 1985 Season; Proyecto Rio Azul, Informe Tres: 1985* (R. E. W. Adams, ed.): 161–167. University of Texas at San Antonio, San Antonio.
1987b  Ten Phonetic Syllables. *Research Reports on Ancient Maya Writing* 14. Center for Maya Research, Washington, D.C.
1988a  Blood Symbolism in Maya Iconography. In *Maya Iconography* (Elizabeth P. Benson and Gillett Griffin, eds.): 175–221. Princeton University Press, Princeton.
1988b  The Rio Azul Cacao Pot: Epigraphic Observations on the Function of a Maya Ceramic Vessel. *Antiquity* 62: 153–157.
1990   A New Decipherment of "Directional Count" Glyphs. *Ancient Mesoamerica* 1 (2): 213–224.
n.d.a  Epigraphic Evidence of Political Organization in the Usumacinta Drainage. Unpublished ms., 1984.
n.d.b  Readings with the Syllable *tsa.* Unpublished ms., 1990.

STUART, GEORGE E.
1981   Maya Art Treasures Discovered in Cave. *National Geographic* 160 (2): 220–235.

TEDLOCK, DENNIS (TRANS.)
1985   *Popol Vuh: The Definitive Edition of the Mayan Book of the Dawn of Life and the Glories of Gods and Kings.* Simon and Schuster, New York.

THOMAS, CYRUS
1888   Aids to the Study of the Maya Codices. *Sixth Annual Report of the Bureau of Ethnology (1884–1885):* 253–371. Smithsonian Institution, Washington, D.C.

THOMPSON, J. ERIC S.
1937   *A New Method of Deciphering Yucatecan Dates with Special Reference to Chichen Itza.* Carnegie

Institution of Washington, Pub. 483; Contribution 22. Washington, D.C.

1950 *Maya Hieroglyphic Writing: An Introduction.* Carnegie Institution of Washington, Pub. 589. Washington, D.C.

1962 *A Catalog of Maya Hieroglyphs.* University of Oklahoma Press, Norman.

1972 A Commentary on the Dresden Codex. *Memoirs of the American Philosophical Society* 59. Philadelphia.

TOWNSEND, RICHARD F.

1982 Pyramid and Sacred Mountain. In *Ethnoastronomy and Archaeoastronomy in the American Tropics* (Anthony Aveni and Gary Urton, eds.): 37–62. Annals of the New York Academy of Sciences 385. New York Academy of Sciences, New York.

VILLACORTA C., J. ANTONIO, and CARLOS A. VILLACORTA

1930 *Códices mayas.* Tipografía Nacional, Guatemala.

VOGT, EVON

1976 *Tortillas for the Gods: A Symbolic Analysis of Zinacanteco Rituals.* Harvard University Press, Cambridge.